READING THOMAS HARDY

This major new reading of the novels of Thomas Hardy by leading critic George Levine disentangles the author's often elaborately distanced prose from his beautiful poetic and precise renderings of the natural world. Clear, direct, and minimally academic in his own writing, Levine provides an overview of Hardy's entire fictional canon, with extensive discussions of his early and late novels including his last, *The Well-Beloved*. In so doing Levine draws new attention to the way Hardy absorbed both the ideas and the writing strategies of Charles Darwin, and develops new perspectives first articulated in the literary responses of Virginia Woolf and D. H. Lawrence. Levine departs from the critical norm by reading Hardy in the context of his deep feeling for the natural world and all living things, and the implicit affirmation of life that sometimes drives his bleakest narratives.

GEORGE LEVINE, professor emeritus of English, Rutgers University, has published broadly on Victorian topics, including *Darwin and the Novelists* (1988), *How to Read the Victorian Novel* (2007), and the award-winning *Realism, Ethics and Secularism: Essays on Victorian Literature and Science* (Cambridge, 2008). He is editor of *The Cambridge Companion to George Eliot* (Cambridge, 2001) and was co-editor of the journal *Victorian Studies* in its early years.

READING WRITERS AND THEIR WORK

READING THOMAS HARDY

GEORGE LEVINE

Rutgers University, New Jersey

CAMBRIDGE
UNIVERSITY PRESS

University Printing House, Cambridge CB2 8BS, United Kingdom

One Liberty Plaza, 20th Floor, New York, NY 10006, USA

477 Williamstown Road, Port Melbourne, VIC 3207, Australia

314-321, 3rd Floor, Plot 3, Splendor Forum, Jasola District Centre, New Delhi - 110025, India

79 Anson Road, #06-04/06, Singapore 079906

Cambridge University Press is part of the University of Cambridge.

It furthers the University's mission by disseminating knowledge in the pursuit of education, learning and research at the highest international levels of excellence.

www.cambridge.org
Information on this title: www.cambridge.org/9781316630808
DOI: 10.1017/9781316823293

© George Levine 2017

First published 2017

A catalogue record for this publication is available from the British Library

ISBN 978-1-107-17796-3 Hardback
ISBN 978-1-316-63080-8 Paperback

For Marge, one more time, who left me too soon
For Rachel who held me together
With a loving Hardyan nod to her canine and feline
assistants, Lucy and Trixie

Contents

Preface

I

Why return, as readers have long been doing, to the bleak, dark, intensely pessimistic novels of Thomas Hardy? This book is my perhaps too personal answer to that question, representing a lifetime of changing engagement with the novels. There is something about Hardy's writing (sometimes, of course, not always) that transcends his excessive and defensive pessimism. His great novels have a peculiar vitality and power even as they seem to express a dark vision of some great evolutionary mistake, in which consciousness is a painful anomaly and individual lives are helplessly bound by a nature entirely indifferent, if not overtly hostile. Hardy the novelist has emerged from my lifelong engagement with him as a writer whose passion for art is a reflex of his passion for nature and of his sometimes bewildered recognition that something so beautiful, so abundant, so subtle, so vast is also inimical to the life for which he felt an almost universal compassion. It made him one of the great poets of life, attuned to its subtlest manifestations and uncannily alert to its abundant variations and significances. And so I want to offer here an almost celebratory reading of an alternative Hardy, one who can transform our perception of life and affirm it even in his dogmatic pessimism and his dramatization of its inevitable disasters and more than "little" ironies.

As an adolescent aspirant to serious literary criticism, I thought Hardy's novels weren't sophisticated enough. Their language was too often ponderously abstract and polysyllabic; their pervasive pessimism seemed to me too easy – I was, after all, an English major. Their diagrammatic manipulation of plots to make all things come out for the worst seemed too crude, though I was proud, in my sophistication, of being myself a thoroughly pessimistic sort of fellow. D. H. Lawrence, whose posthumously published "Study of Thomas Hardy" will be one of my constant points of reference throughout this book, was on my side: he puts it rather aggressively, "it is

ix

not as a metaphysician that one must consider Hardy . . . nothing in his work is so pitiable as his clumsy efforts to push events into line with his theory of being, and to make calamity fall on those who represent the principle of Love" (*P*, p. 480). In spite of the impressive effort at that time of Albert Guerard to enlist Hardy, along with Conrad, in the ranks of twentieth-century modernism, Hardy's writing seemed to run counter to the ideal of art against which I had been learning to judge him: twentieth-century modernism's austere, complex, psychologically intense, sometimes cryptic experimentalism. The novels were anything but psychological studies, and, really, did Tess's note have to slip under the rug? Or, in *A Pair of Blue Eyes*, did Elfride's earring really have to fall off during her awkward first kiss? And what was I to do with that grossly, exaggeratedly Malthusian figure of the child, little Father Time, in *Jude the Obscure*?

But an odd thing happened on the way to where I am today, geriatrically enlightened and perhaps too eagerly appreciative. Hardy got subtler, smarter, more sensitive, his novels richer and more moving. Hardy, it turns out, was not an awkward realist but a poet of a new way – a post-Darwinian way – of looking at the world. He was in touch with energies that the modernists, on the one hand, and the Victorian writers I was coming to love, on the other, did not by and large try to touch. His tendency not to dwell on the workings of the minds of his protagonists and to focus with almost symbolic intensity on the material objects that shape their world, his rejection of the happy-ending plot, and his symmetrical, almost mathematical manipulation of events turned out to be much more than simple ironic perversions of Victorian ideals. They were not only aspects of his determinedly artful, experimental, and nonrealist engagement with new Victorian understandings of nature and of mind; they were representations of deeply felt responses to this new world. The same D. H. Lawrence who condemned Hardy's philosophizing and plot manipulation found in Hardy a remarkable and daring visionary:

> His feeling, his instinct, his sensuous understanding is, however, apart from his metaphysic, very great and deep, deeper than that, perhaps, of any other English novelist. Putting aside his metaphysic, which must always obtrude when he thinks of people, and turning to the earth, to landscape, then he is true to himself. (*P*, p. 480)

This is my theme, and by the time I wrote the first-written of the essays revised here, on *The Mayor of Casterbridge* (now Chapter 3), I had come to believe that Hardy's writing required a different sort of attention. I needed to account for his work's peculiar power that extended well beyond the tragic, symmetrical stories that climax in the disasters of *Jude the Obscure*; I needed to come to terms with what had seemed to me and many critics contradictory elements in his writing – realism that always threatened to break out of realist constraints; moral conservatism always on the edge of violation; a paradoxical combination of biological determinism with a tendency to write in "a female tradition";[1] intuitive and deeply felt strong representations of vitality and energy, although always thwarted and denied; movingly sympathetic representations of nonhuman forms of life and of objects and landscapes: knowing readings of how nature signifies and demonstrations of nature's meaninglessness. A man who didn't want to be touched fills his novels with lovers who aspire to be touched (and women like Sue Bridehead, of *Jude the Obscure*, who resist touching even after making commitments to their lovers), whose desires drive plots and whose frustrations complete them. Each return to Hardy puzzled me even as it revealed to me new things about his writing and touched me with a new sense of what I can only call elemental feelings. Hardy's writing thrusts me into a beautiful and often violently difficult nature thronging with myriad other kindred beings, and it still moves me in its revelation of the intricacies, variations, and abundance of life.

It wasn't Hardy's dark philosophy that made me return to him so often: I developed new respect for his repeated assertion that he was not a philosopher and was not aiming for any philosophical consistency. My adolescent resistance to the manipulations of plot was not entirely ignorant; it marked an undeveloped awareness of something else, more important, more directly alive than the ideas by which Hardy's mind had been violated. The great power of Hardy lay not in dramatizations of a world we never made but in imaginations of the energies that drive life through all of nature. However derivative his ideas about the world might have been, Hardy was marvelously original when he looked out at that world and found a way to say what he saw. His seeing is infused with feeling, and the world he sees resonates with meaning.

Trying to account for what it is that makes Hardy so essential a novelist despite the obvious limitations I have suggested entailed for me a new look at old materials. I wanted to find a way to the Hardy who transcends his own philosophically dark vision by considering how he looks with unique intensity and precision at nature in all its forms. I wanted to represent a Hardy who dramatizes in every novel the way art transforms into meaning the tangled and mindless nature that he sees so precisely and so relentlessly. He claimed that novel writing was always compromised by the marketplace, but that his real vocation, his real love, was poetry. It is true that Hardy's novels belong in the great tradition of English fiction, but their greatest power is in what I will be calling their poetry.

From the perspective of this book, Hardy's particular greatness as a novelist emerges most prominently in those sequences that may seem gratuitous if one focuses only on the movement of story, but that demand attention because of their own remarkable attention to the world that lies outside of the story a novel can tell. His writing in these sequences achieves the condition of poetry and, ironically perhaps, gives story its best life.[2] They depend on the local perspective employed in the passages, either that of a character or of the narrator himself; they entail radical shifts of attention from a central dramatic situation to an ambient world, often otherwise unobserved, sometimes caught by chance, out of the corner of a protagonist's eye, but always there in the eye of the narrator himself. In the last chapter, I will linger over several such sequences. These are the moments when Hardy breaks free of the constraints of the conventions of Victorian novel-writing within which he felt himself bound – it is when Hardy becomes most distinctively himself.

The poetry of his novels emerges as the prose twists away from story and from Hardy's philosophical revulsion from a world he never made – vast beyond human limits, subject to relentlessly unfeeling laws of growth and struggle, decay and death. That world, abstractly or even allegorically represented, is dark indeed, but there can be a breathtaking beauty in Hardy's writing about it. These passages reimagine the relation and the continuities between the human that makes for fictional narrative and the "natural."

There is a life that throbs through many of the novels that only a few recent critics have engaged. "Alongside the doomed sense of weighted past and incipient conclusion," Gillian Beer has argued, "goes a sense of plenitude, and 'appetite for joy.'"[3] In this book, I am looking for the Hardy whom Beer has claimed to find, and I find him represented best by two novelists: Lawrence and Virginia Woolf. Reading Hardy with novelists' eyes, they head straight for what is most original and vital. They recognize in Hardy a Darwinian way of looking at the world. Hardy's writing not only embodies his bleak interpretation of what Darwin argued, but it contains as well something of Darwin's meticulousness of description and emotional absorption in the tangled life he so scrupulously watched. The Darwin who helped shape Hardy's way of looking at the world had the eye of a poet and of a novelist as well as of a scientist. He looked at the world with an intensity and precision that could have been inspired only by an enormous appetite for nature. So, as in chapter after chapter I invoke Lawrence and Woolf, Darwin must take a chapter to himself. There I discuss not so much Darwin's theories as his ways of seeing and describing the natural world. Elsewhere I have argued that with no illusions about the processes by which nature grinds out life through death, Darwin also finds the world extraordinarily beautiful, even enchanting.[4] So while Hardy certainly took Darwin's theory as scientific confirmation of nature's indifference to human desire and intelligence, he found in the procedures of Darwin's prose a spur to explore nature's working with microscopic intensity and telescopic imagination. Moreover, he took Darwin's arguments to imply that humans have deep moral obligations not only to other humans, but to the whole world of conscious beings.

I make no claims that the understanding of Hardy that drives this book is new, only that it has not had an adequate hearing in the criticism. Lawrence's extraordinary rhapsody, "A Study of Thomas Hardy," despite its almost mystical pages of theories about life and sex, has been my primary influence here. Lawrence reads Hardy with a deeply personal engagement and in so doing focuses on just the most original and exciting aspects of Hardy's work. The "Study" is so far from the norm of recent Hardy criticism that I have felt a bit uneasy about finding it so revelatory and so useful;[5] it nevertheless seems to me to capture the greatness of Hardy's novels as well as anyone ever has.

Lawrence's intimate, living relation to the novels themselves is liberating, and almost completely incompatible with the main line of current criticism. The readings might be condemned now as too personally engaged with the characters in Hardy's novels, as though they were real people not fictions. The current term of art to describe such criticism is "characterological." But Lawrence's Hardy, flaws and all, leaps into life off his pages. Lawrence's Hardy struggles with the social conventions that Lawrence fought more overtly. In Hardy's profound sensitivity to the forces of nature, Lawrence finds what he thinks of as Hardy's distinctive contribution to the "one bright book of life."

Not coincidentally, the criticism of another early twentieth-century novelist evokes a similar Hardy. Although the difference between Lawrence and Virginia Woolf might have made one anticipate antagonistic understandings, Woolf's gorgeous essay on Hardy, subsequently published in her *English Common Reader*, gets at what might be called the Lawrentian heart of the matter. Sensitive to Hardy's remarkable powers of description of nature, she notes that "He is aware in a larger sense of Nature as a force; he feels in it a spirit that can sympathize or mock or remain the indifferent spectator of Human fortunes." His stories, she says, are "watched by the eyes of the gods and worked out in the presence of Nature" (*VW*, p. 223). In listing the great distinguishing qualities of Hardy's art, Woolf claims that "more than any other novelist," Hardy "brings before us" "a sense of the physical world . . . the sense that the little prospect of man's existence is ringed by a landscape which, while it exists apart, yet confers a deep and solemn beauty upon his drama" (225). Once again, it takes a novelist to get to the heart of the Hardyan matter.

And finally, there is the word of Hardy himself, in which he makes explicit the connection between the work art does and the conditions that prevail in nature, a connection that I will try to elaborate in this book's last two chapters:

> So, then, if Nature's defects must be looked in the face and transcribed, whence arises the *art* in poetry and novel-writing? Which must certainly show art, or it becomes merely mechanical reporting. I think the art lies in making these defects the basis of a hitherto unperceived beauty, by irradiating them with "the light that never was" on their surface, but is seen to be latent in them by the spiritual eye. (*LWTW*, p. 118)

II

In this book, I am taking as exemplary of the wrong kind of Hardy the notorious sequence about little Father Time in *Jude the Obscure*, in which Jude's young son kills himself and all of Jude's other children. There is something tendentious and merely philosophical in the extravagant excess of it all. It is the most famous example of the way Hardy's plots often strain, with whatever devices he can seize upon, toward the fulfillment of a preplanned disaster. Lawrence characterizes such plot developments, not entirely unfairly, as morality plays. But Hardy is a greater writer hiding in plain sight, hunkered down behind a barricade of respectability and philosophical profundities, the disguised author of his own official biography, a doggedly reputable figure whose novels demonstrate anything but respect for the respectability he sought. This other Hardy, always full of contradictions, imagines a world driven by chance but represented in forms almost symmetrically shaped (as when Jude and Sue in *Jude the Obscure* virtually trade their positions in regard to religion and morality). This Hardy is an almost natural writer who unfortunately also often clogs his prose with evidences of respectability and learning; he is a lover of life and the living, yet committed to plotting a world into which it would have been better not to have been born. The poetry I am emphasizing emerges unexpectedly from page to page, often seemingly against the grain of the plots. In the first chapter I try to address this peculiar contradiction in Hardy, the pull to respectability, which Lawrence despised, and the deep love and admiration for forces of nature that are anything but respectable. One can see that tension played out in the center of the plot of *The Mayor of Casterbridge*, which I discuss in that respect in a later chapter.

The urgency with which I have come in this book to rethink and reexperience Hardy derives partly from my sense that the great burst of theory-saturated criticism of the last few decades,[6] even as it has often brilliantly sustained Hardy's position in the pantheon of English novelists and enriched awareness of the depth and complexity of his relentless narratives of loss and death, does not do justice to the Woolfian, the Lawrentian Hardy. The Hardy I have engaged here is the writer of extraordinary nature poems in the midst of complicated Victorian narratives, poems in which Hardy observes with Darwinian eyes, detecting the most minute movements of life in nature, reading traces of history in rocks and landscapes, dust and mud and leaves and trees, affirming a natural and instinctive life that persists as counterpoint to (sometimes intersecting with) his dramatic narratives of thwarted love and class distinctions. Most of the novels imply what I will be calling an "understory," in which the little moral dramas are expanded in time in a world where things are endlessly interconnected. Hardy requires, in representing that world, new modes of attention: "setting behind the small action of his protagonists the terrific action of unfathomed nature." His constant concern with off-angle perceptions, with the crucial importance of "seeing," observing, zooming and focusing in, is the requisite for this expanded understanding of what constitutes the real, and reshapes what is peripheral into what is central.

Reading Hardy requires as much attention to what might be thought of as mere context or "background description" as to the unfolding of story. Hardy was certainly a tale teller but even as his protagonists' fates spin downward, the world they occupy persists in its robust alternative life. The poetry notices not only the losses and failures and frustrations of the protagonists, but the violence and vitality of the world that surrounds them: in *Far from the Madding Crowd*, Gabriel Oak's sheep are led over a cliff by a sweet young dog that will have to be killed for its error; in *Tess* there is a horse pierced and bleeding to death; in *Jude* there is a trapped rabbit screaming; and almost everywhere in Hardy's novels, we learn of snails whose shells seem always cracking underfoot, sleeping doves tumbling into the fire, moths crackling in the candle flame, sometimes as signals between lovers, fossils evoking epochs of extinction. Trees grind moaning against each other, violent storms and fires destroy or change directions of lives, stars and meteors dizzyingly distant from their awed and shrinking observers play out dramas of movement sublimely beyond human capacity for feeling, at the very limits of human perception and understanding.

The novels are alive with delicate and precise images of ephemera, like moths and slugs and gnats and snails and birds and glowworms and leaves, registering freshly the busyness, intricacy, and profusion of life. These often tiny forms of life may seem from moment to moment mere backdrops to the human dramas with which the novels are primarily concerned – social manners, fine class distinctions, anxieties about morals, love, and money as they depend on and clash with each other. But the understories are far more than backdrop; they play out active elements essential to Hardy's imagined world, where the human dramas, driven by improbable twists of Chance, are chancy only to the conventional perceptions that Hardy's narratives attempt to transcend. As Woolf insisted, the human drama is inevitably entangled with lives and forces other than human. Hardy's writerly eyes detect these lives and forces everywhere, and their existence inflects the tone and feeling of his Victorian dramas and melodramas. But even as the novels give shape to reality so as to reverse the patterns of the usual Victorian plots, they do not make moral sense of the world. Driven by hypersensitivity to all forms of life and by compassion for individual human suffering in a world he never made, Hardy evokes in the novels alternate narratives, understories, usually fragmentarily revealed. One might well experience them as life-affirming.

The true morality of Hardy's novels is in the life they shadow forth on the margins of drama and melodrama, a life represented with extraordinary originality and sensitivity. The morality is in the distinctiveness of Hardy's art – the great defense against the off-angle forces of society and nature that attempt to impose moral norms on an experience always too wild and vital to be contained. It is the art that gives shape and meaning, exploiting the Darwinian powers of finding life in the most obscure places, and reading meaning in apparent randomness, history in every object.

The counterpoint makes for painful harmony, a re-imagination of reality, often startling both in its revelations and in its beauty. The abundance and complexity of the world, its very refusal to bend to the desires of the humans who make themselves protagonists, is a recurring motif in Hardy's novels. Hardy's art might be taken as the work of finding order and meaning in that abundance and apparent randomness, as it were, scouring the fields with Tess to find the obscure garlic hidden in the grass.

It makes something beautiful of mindless processes and hopelessly complex entanglements. This enterprise is intimated as early as Hardy's first and extravagant novel, *Desperate Remedies*, whose epigraph is from Walter Scott: "Though an unconnected course of adventure is what most frequently occurs in nature, yet the province of the romance-writer being artificial, there is more required from him than a mere compliance with the simplicity of reality" (*DR*).

Not that reality is really simple. Hardy would have remembered Darwin daringly affirming, after the most elaborate exposition of complicated connections, "not that in nature the relations can ever be as simple as this" (*OS*, p. 73). The "simplicity" is rather apparent randomness, working like Darwin's natural selection, not according to some intelligent design (like the design of the romancer) but according to the possibilities allowed by the rigid laws of nature within the totally contingent, accidental conditions of the moment. The simplicity is entanglement, a complexity so enormous that its interconnections are not intelligible except through the cunning of science or the artifices of art.

I will be insisting throughout that a major aspect of Hardy's novels is his art of hearing the counter melodies and writing the understory. He regularly shifts focus and alerts attention. He attends to the limits of particular perspectives (as Hardy recognized that astronomy had to do and was doing in his own time), of seeing what's on the periphery, of coming to terms with a world always in motion, so charged with life and movement and physical energy that any single "story" would be inadequate and has to be recognized as part of something larger, impersonal, and aimless. That "reality" remains fundamentally indifferent to the human desires that make for the beginnings, middles, and ends of story. The capacity to hear that counter melody, to read the understory of these phenomena, is one of the distinguishing marks of Hardy's narrators and the occasional keen-eyed protagonists who, like Giles Winterborne of *The Woodlanders*, suffer for their perceptions. At one point in *Desperate Remedies*, in one of those sage discussions among minor rural figures who populate the Wessex novels, Farmer Springrove and his friend are discussing death. Fatalists both, they yet register what I take to be one of the central aspects of Hardy's art. A surprising death, in fact any sudden unlikely event, Springrove says, "is just a discovery of your own mind, and not an alteration in the Lord's" (ch. 21, p. 450). The "Lord's" intention is the adamant (if vital) reality governed by irreversible laws that we dream beyond, that we plan beyond, that we fail to see (often until it is too late), and that we imagine are malleable. Our subjectivities miss what is adamant and irresistible about the world out there in favor of what we desire out there to be like. There is after all no "Chance" in Hardy's chance-saturated world – the rules of the world do not change; our minds at their keenest, at their most artful, come to notice them and make art of them.

Hardy's novels are, then, novels of vision, or, perhaps more precisely, novels of sensibility. Even when the plots point predictably downward, their worlds tingle along the edges of perception. The novels engage a fundamentally nonhuman world too abundant and complicated to be contained; they are alert to what ordinary life overlooks but that is intrinsic to it. They become shaping narratives of discovery even if the protagonists cannot make those discoveries themselves, and they evoke, in their darkest moments, compassion for the living figures who are doomed both by society and by the laws of nature.

Like so much other Victorian literature, like the science that Hardy read and followed, his novels – as the critic and sage John Ruskin put it in a very different context – not only teach his readers how to see but also suggest the overwhelming urgency of seeing. A keen observer can discover the phenomena at work even before they occasionally and catastrophically impinge on the course of human affairs. The narrator and in fragmentary ways the protagonists infer significance from every object, for objects are rarely merely objects – they are histories, intimations of unseen life, hints at improbable connections in a Darwinian world in which everything is related to everything else, and all things have deep histories. The visible world, the sensibly accessible world, is charged with life and meaning, as it is in Darwin's prose as well; but it must be seen, and it might be said that Hardy's novels teach us to see it. History is built into the present. It is readable in rocks and ruins, in faces and bodies, in stars and in insects, even in dust. The present is incomprehensible without it. Art is a crucial means of discovery.

The fragmentary plots of ephemera and vastness are implicitly juxtaposed with human drama, more or less Victorian-realist in texture; unlike the realist plots, radically unlike Hardy's own plots, these parallel phenomena are without beginning, middle, and end – saturated with history and always happening. Their presence, marginal to the perceptions of most of the protagonists, poetically and critically essential to the narrator, is intrinsic to the Victorian dramas that play out in the world that they too occupy. While Hardy does not pause to moralize them, his practice of evoking the details of their reality implies something of the way George Eliot famously put it: "If we had a keen vision and feeling of ordinary human life, it would be like hearing the grass grow and the squirrel's heart beat, and we should die of that roar which lies on the other side of silence."[7] Mistaken for George Eliot in his earliest novels, Hardy fills his own with passages that record the other side of silence.

Hardy's extraordinary attentiveness to the multiplicities and particularities and significances of nature is the strongest evidence for my larger argument, that he is far more loving of this theoretically cruel world than he is normally taken to be. Hardy may not be an original thinker, but he is an original "seer." His acts of attention to the worlds in which his protagonists move are, as in the writings of his much admired Darwin, acts of love; Hardy's world reverberates with significances that only the finest sensibilities of his characters and the apparently detached consciousness of his narrators can detect. No English novelist is as sensitive to the abundance and complexity of the natural world. It might seem ironic, but just that sensitivity pushes Hardy to focus on the centrality of human consciousness. For it is the extraordinary power of that consciousness that makes it possible for little human beings to range between the vast realities of the starry universe and the minutiae of insect life with equal comprehension – and with awe.

So there is an irony in the directions Hardy's fictions take that parallels the irony of the implications of Darwin's own ostensibly materialist thinking. The unthinking, indifferent natural world has somehow produced a creature capable of thinking and of recognizing that world's incapacity to think at all. The express tension in Hardy between the natural world and the consciousnesses that suffer from being able to see it and think about it requires him, after all, to dramatize consciousness itself, in all its paradoxical tensions. His detached narrators look down on the experience they narrate from a great height. But they have insight into it that the characters themselves, by and large, do not; they call our attention to things that, as mere thinking participants, we could not see on our own. As the consciousness of characters within the narratives expands, the pain of knowing grows. Apparently not a psychological writer for whom the action is thrown inside, he produces novels of considerable psychological complexity, leaving it to the reader to understand the implications of actions and events and things; the world of things implies a world of consciousness perceiving them, and, indeed, a world elsewhere.

The idea of a world mindlessly created and run, aimlessly in motion, regardless of human desires, certainly was crucial to Hardy's famous pessimism, but it was also crucial to his ambivalence about human consciousness and sensitivities. These make his protagonists exceptionally vulnerable to pain, but they also make the art that creates them possible.

Darwin also lies behind Hardy's expressed and dramatized compassion for virtually all living things, for we are all quite literally related, we are all similarly entitled to attention and care. Heightened attention and shifts of focus are Darwinian attributes as well; these strategies allow Hardy to represent the external world, the world that is not inside us, in ways that invoke inwardness after all. The power to recognize and represent that external world, that nature of intricate entanglements, becomes both the most distinctive human power and the means to the fullest extension of what I will sentimentally characterize as love. At the heart of virtually all of Hardy's strategies of defense, imaginations of disaster, and imaginations of vitality lies Darwinian thinking and feeling.

The world is readable as Darwin read it: all things are creatures of time who leave their traces and intimate important histories; the world is mindless and all modes of order (including Hardy's almost obsessive way of ordering his narratives neatly) are artful human impositions on an entangled nature; nature is entirely indifferent to human desire; human intelligence and sensibility in their fullest development outleap their adaptive functions. Developments out of natural selection, they both give humans the advantage in the struggles for existence and make them particularly vulnerable to the indifference and complexity of the forces of nature. And yet they are the condition for the creation of order and of art. Hardy invents a strategy of narration (embodied often thematically in the novels) that keeps him as narrator invulnerable as he reveals the richness and dangerousness of the ambient world. Hidden behind the orders of his language, he tells stories of figures who dare to follow the irrational orders of their feelings, and who are thus admirably doomed. Art is something Hardy hides behind. It is also an opening to life. It is the life in Hardy that matters most.

Acknowledgments

This book was originally conceived as a gathering of my essays on Hardy sprinkled through the years. It became quite another thing, a new argument about Hardy. Some of the materials, large pieces and small, are scattered throughout this book:

"Thomas Hardy's the *Mayor of Casterbridge*: Reversing the Real," *The Realistic Imagination* (Chicago: University of Chicago Press, 1981), ch. 11, pp. 229–251.

"The Cartesian Hardy: I Think Therefore I Am Doomed," *Dying to Know* (Chicago: University of Chicago Press, 2002), ch. 9, pp. 200–219.

"Shaping Hardy's Art: Vision, Class, and Sex," in John Richetti, ed., *Columbia History of the Novel* (New York: Columbia University Press, 1994), pp. 533–559.

"Hardy and Darwin: An Enchanting Hardy?" in Keith Wilson, ed., *A Companion to Thomas Hardy* (Wiley-Blackwell, 2009), pp. 36–53

"Hardy's 'Inward Turn': From Mindless Matter to the Art of the Mind," *The Hardy Review*, 15 No. 2 (2013), pp. 11–26.

Abbreviations

Below is a list of novels and critical studies to which reference is frequently made in the course of this book. With each entry, I provide an abbreviation that will facilitate reference in the text. The editions of Hardy's novels listed here are sound but very various, for they are the ones with which I have regularly worked and which I have used in teaching. The date in brackets is the date of original publication. In the text, I accompany page numbers with chapter numbers so that the quotations may be found in any of the many other editions of Hardy's novels now available.

Charles Darwin, *On the Origin of Species: A Facsimile of the First Edition* (Cambridge, MA: Harvard University Press, 1964), *OS*.

Thomas Hardy, *Desperate Remedies* (London: Macmillan and Co, Ltd., 1926 [1871]), *DR*.

Thomas Hardy, *Under the Greenwood Tree* (London: Penguin Books, 1985 [1872]), *UGW*.

Thomas Hardy, *A Pair of Blue Eyes* (London: Macmillan, 1975 [1873]), *PBE*.

Thomas Hardy, *Far from the Madding Crowd* (Boston: Riverside Press, 1957 [1874]), *FM*.

Thomas Hardy, *The Hand of Ethelberta: A Comedy in Chapters* (London: Macmillan, 1905 [1876]), *HE*.

Thomas Hardy, *The Return of the Native* (London: Penguin Books, 1982 [1878]), *RN*.

Thomas Hardy, *The Trumpet Major* (London: Macmillan, 1974 [1880]), *TM*.

Thomas Hardy, *Two on a Tower* (London: Macmillan, 1975 [1882]), *TT*.

Thomas Hardy, *The Mayor of Casterbridge: A Study of a Man of Character* (New York: W. W. Norton and Co, 1977 [1886]), *MC*.

Thomas Hardy, *The Woodlanders* (The New Wessex Edition) (London: Macmillan, 1974 [1887]), *W*.

Thomas Hardy, *Tess of the d'Urbervilles* (Oxford: Oxford University Press, 1988 [1891]), *TD*.

Thomas Hardy, *Jude the Obscure* (London: Penguin Books, 1978 [1895]), *JO*.

Thomas Hardy, *The Well-Beloved: A Sketch of a Temperament* (Oxford: Oxford World Classics, 1991[1897]), *WB*.

Thomas Hardy, *Literary Notebooks of Thomas Hardy*, ed. Lennart A. Björk (New York: New York University Press, 1985), *LN*.

D. H. Lawrence, "A Study of Thomas Hardy," in *Phoenix: The Posthumous Papers of D. H. Lawrence* (New York: The Viking Press, 1936), *P*.

Michael Millgate, *Thomas Hardy: His Career as a Novelist* (New York: Random House, 1971), *MMTH*.

Michael Millgate, *Thomas Hardy: A Biography* (New York: Random House, 1982), *MMB*.

Michael Millgate, ed., *The Life and Work of Thomas Hardy* (Athens, OH: University of Georgia Press, 1985), *LWTH*.

J. Hillis Miller, *Thomas Hardy: Distance and Desire* (Cambridge, MA: The Belknap Press, Harvard University Press, 1970), *DD*.

Virginia Woolf, "Thomas Hardy," in *The Second Common Reader* (New York: Harcourt, Brace and World, 1960 [1932]), *VW*.

CHAPTER I

Shaping Hardy's Art
Vision, Class, and Sex

The cruelest man living could not sit at his feast unless he sat blindfold.

Ruskin, Unto This Last

In a world where the blind only are cheerful we should all do well to put out our eyes.

Hardy, The Hand of Ethelberta

He entered on rational considerations of what a vast gulf lay between that lady and himself, what a troublesome world it was to live in where such divisions could exist, and how painful was the evil when a man of his unequal history was possessed of a keen sensibility.

Hardy, "An Indiscretion in the Life of an Heiress"

I

In order to appreciate adequately the sort of enchantment that Hardy's art casts over otherwise so dark a world, one has to come to terms with its overt and considered life-denying implications. Critics have long noted the Schopenhauerian aspects of Hardy's fiction, the idea that it would be better not to have been born, which is played out so gruesomely in the suicide of little Father Time in *Jude*. But this is only half the story, for Hardy's Schopenhauerian gloom should be recognized as the consequence of an intense feeling *for* life. Confronting the emotional blankness of a world absolutely indifferent to human consciousness and sensibility, and a world of social restraints that punishes the very animal desires that are the conditions for survival, Hardy implicitly affirms those desires through his extraordinary feeling for the textures of the natural world.

In the stories he tells, the pains Hardy feared dominate the pleasures that might be reaped. His "elemental" resistance to life is the other side of his elemental and extreme passion for it, a sensibility that manifests itself in his pervasive preoccupation with "seeing." He sees what is beautiful but recognizes as well the innumerable ways in which life does damage to the sensibility that is, ironically, its product. Seeing acutely brings to the attention of readers a world abundant in forms of life that Hardy's protagonists themselves only occasionally glimpse, intent as they are on their loves and lives. The "life" in Hardy's novels – robust, prolific, various – is registered from perspectives that resist the pain acuteness of vision inflicts. The more you know, the more you can be hurt, but the more you know, the more wonderful the world can seem. Hardy's strong feeling for life is most evident in the way his pages at their most powerful are full of vital things not apparently central to the story. While his prose registers the shame and humiliation that social forces, always ready to punish and disgrace, inflict on those below, on those who yield to sexual vitality or who aspire to conditions beyond those into which they were born, it registers as well the vital force that makes so much of the world (dangerously) attractive.

So the texture of Hardy's writing paradoxically affirms the world that it officially denies. Its careful attention to the things of this world implies feelings of attachment, even of love (which leave him particularly vulnerable). His "keen sensibility" generates perceptions, tensions, and contradictions that can be more interesting and more moving than the doom-ridden plots and often heavy philosophizing that are their frequent vehicle. Pleasure in description of the physical world itself is accompanied by anxiety about the dangers of indulging the sensibility that makes the pleasure possible. No longer believing in any but the material world and skeptical about what can be assuredly known there, he dramatizes desire and hides from it in a new aesthetic austerity. Self-discipline keeps one respectable and becomes a condition for survival in a world that crushes the miraculous capacities of seeing, knowing, and feeling that it created. "Seeing" becomes the supreme virtue as it is the supreme danger – it allows one to know without being touched; but it also allows one to know too much.

Lawrence was drawn to Hardy's willingness to engage unconventional vital forces; he was disappointed by Hardy's desperate aspiration to respectability and his unwillingness to take the full risk of that engagement:

> [R]emain quite within the convention, and you are good, safe, and happy in the long run, though you never have the vivid pang of sympathy on your side: or, on the other hand, be passionate, individual, willful, you will find the security of the convention a walled prison, you will escape, and you will die … This is the tragedy … [:] first [that man] is a member of the community, and must, upon his honour, in no way move to disintegrate

the community … second, that the convention of the community is
a prison to his natural, individual desire, a desire that compels him, whether
he feel justified or not, to break the bounds of the community, lands him
outside the pale. (*P*, p. 411)

In Hardy's novels sensuous responsiveness is constrained by social
contingency. His acute powers of observation complicate his attitudes
toward the class structures that govern society and the powerful sexual
drives that govern human behavior. Seen, if at all, out the corners of the
protagonists' eyes, in what I am calling an "understory," nonhuman worlds
counterpoint the central preoccupations of his plots – the interplay of class
and sex. Everything in Hardy's metaphysically meaningless world is, under
keen eyes, charged with meaning and belies the human social organizations
and moral conventions that ostensibly contain it. The observer himself is
likely being observed. There are no secrets in this world, only the desire to
keep them.

The biggest secret is sexuality, which is nevertheless almost always
exposed to others' observation. Sexuality is the greatest obstacle to the
class aspirations to which Hardy and his Ethelberta aspire. He was thus
forced into dramatic self-contradiction, writing of the terrible injustice and
unnaturalness of class distinctions and the absurdity of human conventions
of respectability against the gorgeous and usually ferocious energies and
abundance of life, and at the same time personally struggling to achieve
respectability at all costs – usually through evasiveness and disguise (as
when he wrote his autobiography under his wife Emma's name). Vision
dramatizes the seductiveness of sexuality and nature and at the same time
their power to compromise and elude him. It forces him and his characters
into self-consciousness. For that reason, his novels are almost invariably
narrated by anonymous figures alert both to natural phenomena large and
small and to the nuances of social mores. The protagonists are damned by
respectability *and* by resistance to it, for convention is not only outside
them like a police force. It is inside them like a conscience.

That conscience, however, usually produces not guilt but shame. Where
the characters themselves feel guilt, whatever the narrator may be implying,
the guilt is unjust and destructive. Sue Bridehead's shuddering return to
Phillotson's bed in *Jude the Obscure* is the best and most disturbing image for
this very Hardyesque quality. By and large, however, his characters are not
guilty in their transgressions – Tess, for the most famous example, is a "pure
woman," although she has been raped and has become a murderess. In effect,
Hardy's plots dramatize his own fear of the kinds of transgressions and

ambitions he allows Michael Henchard in *The Mayor of Casterbridge* – or Eustacia Vye in *Return of the Native*, or even the almost parodic doctor, Fitzpiers, of *The Woodlanders*. Hardy seems ashamed of his own shame, and his novels reflect his ambivalent attitude, in part by focusing so often, with fear and admiration, on those recklessly passionate figures, like Henchard in *The Mayor of Casterbridge*, who intentionally or not risk the respectability that might protect them from the doom that follows upon their desires.

Seeing too intensely, too intensely aware of the consequences of being seen, deeply sympathetic to the outcasts of society (and to the animals and insects that move in and out of the characters' lives), desperate to avoid being himself cast out, passionately in love with the physical world, terrified of its indifference to his passion, Hardy writes his novels in disguise. Their greatest strengths are not in their continuing implicit commentary on social or cosmic issues. Rather, they play out his ambivalence, fusing his powers of vision with his deepest desires and anxieties about social success and sexual union. He risks the limits of convention and in the end – to Lawrence's chagrin – punishes the inevitably flawed protagonists who take that risk.

Hardy was plagued with vision, which invariably reveals much that he did not want to see, in particular his own guilty complicity. With the eye of an architect, a Darwinian, a naturalist, and a novelist, Hardy saw history in objects; he saw how phenomena connect or conflict; he saw life subtly and grandly everywhere; he read society in complexions, patterns of labor in postures, systems of hierarchy in dress. And with the peculiar modern self-consciousness of the late nineteenth century, he wrote in hiding from what he saw, developed strategies of protection, secretly admired what he punished and feared. He hid from and animated with poetic sensibility the dangers of the world that his vision disclosed.

Precise observation links inextricably to questions of class and of sexuality. (I want to emphasize sexuality over gender because the gender and class issues in Hardy seem to develop from direct sexual energy, given as an inevitable natural force that disrupts the narratives.) Class is a determiner of position for both observer and observed; sexual desire provokes intense observation and at the same time constantly threatens the stability of class. That threat seems built into the very texture of Hardy's prose, which, like Jude gazing distantly at "Christminster," often strains against the colloquial in an awkward and self-conscious attempt to prove he belonged among those graduates of Oxford who did not have to write for a living. Such writing, so central to his philosophically burdened narrations of disaster, John Bayley has described as Hardy "on duty."¹ Critically, Hardy has always paid the price for this and has been patronized as an "auto-didact." While Hardy off duty, in touch with the vitality of the living world, is quite another writer, his excessive sensitivity to criticism drives his prose too often, his plots almost always.

Given his implicit rejection of class hierarchies, it is significant that he rarely satirizes them; one does not feel even in *The Hand of Ethelberta* – despite some dissolute and buffoonish aristocrats – the sort of antiaristo-cratic animus one finds in many of Dickens' early novels. Ethelberta, the daughter of a butler, though she marries a formerly dissolute aristocrat, does very well among the rich and noble, who are not satirized or, by and large, condemned. Hardy's attitude toward all these things is further complicated by the fact that he saw writing novels as a way to make a living rather than as an expression of authentic (and entirely respectable) art. Fiction writing is secondary to poetry; such writing is a medium for lying and evasion as well as for representation. It is a salable commodity and constantly subject to misinterpretation and to unintended revelations. One extreme expression of this comes in the figure of the bastard-villain William Dare in *A Laodicean*, who manipulates a photograph to incrimi-nate the innocent protagonist, Somerset. Yet more representative is the way Hardy's narratives are obsessed with spying, overhearing, gossip. Notoriously, his first published novel, *Desperate Remedies*, written in response to the fact that his first novel, "The Poor Man and the Lady," was turned down, is manically loaded with spies spying on spies spying on ... Someone is always watching. One will always be observed and always misunderstood. Hardy is thus fascinated by what happens off stage, where the normal, unlike his narrator and his protagonists, is unselfcon-scious about itself.

Self-consciousness and seeing are complexly interconnected, each visual event shaped in its significance by the degree to which observed and observer are alert to their conditions. Hardy's own great powers of obser-vation and natural description suggest why he is so intensely conscious of the pervasiveness of watching and nature's relentless indifference to what humans see. Seeing does not necessarily empower; it frequently exposes and deceives. Hillis Miller succinctly describes Hardy's goal as trying "to escape from the dangers of direct involvement in life and to imagine himself in a position where he could safely see life as it is without being seen and could report that seeing ... [he] sought to protect himself and to play the role of someone who would have unique access to the truth" (*DD*, p. 43).

The image that best embodies this effort is the "window," for while windows provide an opening between two otherwise alien, distinct, isolated worlds, they also imply incompleteness of connection. One can see through windows, even hear through them, but only rarely – although this too happens in Hardy's work – can one touch through them or directly affect or resist what appears in the frame. (As a man who hated to be touched, Hardy would likely have found windows the best, if necessarily limited, means of connecting with the other.) The window gives access without requiring immediate engagement, allows seeing without being seen. Like writing, seeing has the paradoxical function of allowing close-ups while implying the absence (or distance) of what is seen and described. But while windows seem to focus the visual world, they often allow in more than the viewer wants, and they cannot entirely contain the multiplicity and dangers of the material world outside. The lives of Hardy's characters are as frequently disrupted by their own acts of observation as they are by being spied upon. Like much else in Hardy, the framed scene both represents and evades, makes vulnerable and protects, implies and circumvents, approaches contact and resists it.

Hardy's obsession with detached and distanced observation is also related to the distances established by class; the poor protagonist's only access to a higher social position is through observation – as Jude observes Christminster, as Tess, undetected, observes Angel's comfortable clerical family, as the dying Giles Winterborne, in *The Woodlanders*, preserves his beloved Grace from any questioning of her fidelity to her husband by protectively observing her from outside the window. From the first, as in the never published "Poor Man and the Lady," which seems to have been largely incorporated into the long story "An Indiscretion in the Life of an Heiress," Hardy's novels concentrate thematically on the primary barrier, class, enforced and also threatened by sexuality and ambition. Even *Under the Greenwood Tree* (Fancy and Mr. Maybold) intimates the theme, as does *Far from the Madding Crowd* (Bathsheba and Gabriel), *A Pair of Blue Eyes* (Elfride and Stephen), *Two on a Tower* (Lady Constantine and Swithin), *The Hand of Ethelberta*, *A Laodicean* (Paula Power and Colonel De Stancy, George Somerset), *The Woodlanders* (Giles Winterborne and Grace Melbury), *Tess of the D'Urbervilles* (Tess-Angel-Alec). Even where the obstacles to romance are not primarily class-related, as in *Return of the Native* and *Jude the Obscure*, questions of class are pervasive.

Hardy's Jude-like ambitions make him and his male protagonists susceptible to every seductive Arabella. If the well-beloved Avice of *The Well-Beloved* is endlessly elusive, Tess Durbeyfield is imagined with sensuous particularity. Failures of touching in her novel are dramatized as failures to honor Tess's physical nature, even by Tess herself. Writing, the medium itself, protects the narrator from the catastrophes of sexuality and at the same time describes its irresistible attractiveness; it celebrates the physical and its indulgence and at the same time distances the narrator and reader from it.

As antidote, sexual desire requires restraint from touching. But the difficulties of this are suggested – with almost comic extravagance – by the figure of Colonel De Stancy, in *A Laodicean*, who does in effect renounce touching for years, swears off women entirely, and yet is over-whelmed by desire when he is enticed by his bastard son, Dare, to spy through a little hole in the wall (another kind of window) on the lovely but characteristically elusive Paula Power, exercising in her gymnasium. The peeping colonel might be taken for Hardy himself, though Hardy was aware of the absurdity of his own desires and fears. The patterns of frustration combine a strong sense of sexual energy with a romantic fear of consummation. While Cytherea Graye of *Desperate Remedies* is at last united with her lover, she is one of the rare ones in the Hardy canon. The novels depend on the pattern, sometimes almost symmetrical, of pursuit and frustration, and they regularly refuse the climax in comic union that is characteristic of the Victorian novel in general. In *A Laodicean*, the pursuit across Europe, first of Somerset seeking Paula, then of Paula seeking Somerset, is only a more exaggerated form of Hardy's usual frustration plot. Contingencies characteristic of life itself, misunder-standings, misperceptions, accidents of timing, virtually inexplicable hes-itations will postpone or ultimately deny lovers their opportunity for consummation.

The examples are everywhere. Elfride Swancourt of *A Pair of Blue Eyes* loses her first tepid love, Stephen Smith, and as Tess is rejected by Angel Clare, she is rejected, by Henry Knight, but then marries a third party whom she doesn't love and dies before her two lovers can resume their pursuits. Christopher Julian, having pursued Ethelberta through the entire novel, fails by moments to stop her marriage to the degenerate Lord Montclere; Lady Constantine dies at the instant that Swithin St. Cleve, in *Two on a Tower*, recovering from the shock of finding her looking old, returns to fulfill his promise to marry her; John Loveday, in *The Trumpet Major*, ultimately loses his love, Anne Garland, to his unstable brother, Bob; Geraldine Allenville, after a novella full of diversions and denials, "An Indiscretion in the Life of an Heiress," flees to her lover, Egbert Mayne, only to die before their relationship can be consummated; Giles

Winterborne of *The Woodlanders* watches over Grace Melbury and dies before she can return to him. Such frustrations climax in Hardy's novelistic career with the stories of Angel and Tess, Jude and Sue. Even when some minor consummations are allowed, Hardy is begrudging, so that the marriage of the endlessly patient Diggory Venn to Thomasin Yeobright in *The Return of the Native* is withdrawn in a revealing footnote in which Hardy encourages the reader to "choose between two endings," of which the "more consistent conclusion" is governed by an "austere artistic code" (Bk 6, ch. 3, p. 464). Consummation not only entails a kind of postcoital lapse from passion and disintegration of desire; it also means the dangerous crossing of class boundaries, social impropriety (with attendant punishment), and the thwarting of professional and social ambition.

The transition from seeing (or writing) to engagement, which may well be provoked by observation, is usually the point of crisis and peripety in Hardy, which is one of the reasons that so many of his stories center on those rare moments when seeing gives way to touching: seeing without touching is frustrating, but the consequences of consummation are catastrophic. Desire and ambition in this world are not quite respectable, but distance is the potential instrument of evasion and disguise.

Recognizing these patterns of defense and, in effect, life-denial, however, should not preclude recognition of Hardy's continuing sympathetic engagement with the recklessness of desire pursued, the very energies that will lead to self-destruction. The abandonment is enormously attractive, even to the anxious narrator who maintains his distance at all times. Many of the novels develop as the consequence of some single "lapse" into passion, ambition, or recklessness, though they may emerge as rather mild in modern terms – Elfride's kiss of Stephen Smith in effect generates the plot of *A Pair of Blue Eyes*; Bathsheba's childish valentine to Boldwood leads to something like tragedy in *Far from the Madding Crowd*, as does her succumbing to the magnificently conscienceless sexuality of Sergeant Troy; *Two on a Tower* traces Lady Constantine's fall into passion for the young astronomer, Swithin, and the consequences of that fall. Most notoriously, *The Mayor of Casterbridge* begins with Learlike precipitation as Henchard sells his wife and is thus released into his ambitions: "If I were a free man again I'd be worth a thousand pounds before I'd done o't" (*MC*, ch. 1, p. 9).

While the pattern Hardy establishes suggests a reading of the world that retains at least some shadow of the moral forms available to writers and their culture in preceding eras, in Hardy failure and defeat after moral trespass do not result from the moral order of the universe: it has no moral order. Rather they emerge from the conflict between the mindless natural order itself and the extraordinary human powers to see, to understand and feel, to imagine the ideal. They result also in part from the conflict between desire and the arbitrary restraints of social systems. The asymmetry between desire and social order suggests that the rules and language humans use to deal with the world are not intrinsic to that world, but mere human impositions. In such a Lawrentian world, breaking the rules, abandoning constraint is the reverse of evil; in some ways it is the great ideal. But while it is endlessly desirable it is not "respectable."

While Lawrence is right that Hardy systematically punishes those who break from respectability, it is central to Hardy's achievement that his desire to see without being seen also implies a strong desire to break out of the conventional world to which he feels constrained to submit. It may be the Laodiceans – the lukewarm – who survive in Hardy's world, but it is the Henchards – and even the Sergeant Troys – who win the narratives' deepest engagement. Yet in the long run, the Laodiceans are only a little less likely to suffer disaster than the Henchards. Playing by the rules, as Lawrence's essay insists, is itself life-denying. Moreover, preoccupation with safety and invulnerability rarely means success. One cannot ultimately hide inside the social world that denies desire and vitality. The natural world is not governed by moral Nemesis but by material laws that have no relation to human consciousness except that they may be detected by it. Invulnerability becomes problematic even at moments when the protective distance would seem maximal and is dramatized within the stories themselves in the events and perspectives of the characters. The visual is the formal expression of Hardy's fear of the humiliations of public exposure but also the means that allows him, with the greatest acuity, to register that vital world that he secretly admires and even loves.

The sexuality to which Hardy was reluctantly but inescapably attracted through the simple physical presence of women – who seem in his novels as overwhelmingly attractive as De Stancy found the gymnastic Paula Power – not only threatens social advancement but makes rational control impossible. This real world lies beyond the range of Victorian realism and is ultimately both more important and more powerful than the respectability behind which Hardy regularly hid. Sexuality is the human manifestation of this other, vital, Lawrentian world. More dangerously still, sexuality threatens to break down the strategies of defense by which protagonists seek to keep themselves, like Hardy's narrators, invulnerable. Hardy's dislike of being touched, says Hillis Miller, in his now classic study of Hardy, is fear of ceasing to be a spectator and of being "brought physically into the world of others," and thus "vulnerable to their energy and will. He wanted to remain invisible, untouchable, a disembodied presence able to see without being seen or felt" (Miller, 1970, DD, p. 55).

Many of even the most pedestrian of Hardy's novels contain stunning moments of poetic vision that result from unexpected observations of people or events or natural phenomena. Unsuspectingly observed by acute, surprised, or wary eyes, people and things reveal the secrets of their essential, let us call it "natural," selves. Tom Paulin points to a Hardy sketch for his poem "In a Eweleaze Near Weatherbury," which superimposes a pair of spectacles on a drawing of the leaze, where the poet in his youth had danced with a lover. It is a surreal image, evocative of Magritte both in the stark incompatibility of the human contrivance with the natural landscape and in the transparency of the spectacles, which allows the leaze to show through. Paulin sensibly emphasizes the "random and gratuitous" relationship between spectacles and landscape and the implicitly "anomalous relationship of man to the outer world which is the object of his knowledge."[2] But the image is striking in another way: it implies that everything in the world is under silent scrutiny. Nothing in the almost barren landscape of the leaze – material and unconscious as it is – escapes the narrator's or poet's eye, and nothing is aware that it is being observed.

The image has an almost paranoid quality: what might be discussed comfortably as an epistemological concern must be understood as a tensely emotional one: somebody is watching and ready to expose you. The function of poet and narrator is to observe, and any image of the most profoundly nonhuman landscape is necessarily infected with the self-consciousness of an observer to which the object remains indifferent. "In making even horizontal and clear inspections," he wrote in *Far from the Madding Crowd*, "we colour and mould according to the wants within us whatever our eyes bring in"(*FMC*, ch. 2, p. 14). In the poem Hardy's sketch accompanies, the speaker, Jocelyn-like, feels himself to be precisely who he was when he danced many years before with his lover – "I remain what I was then." The longing for sexuality is there, but an irrepressible self-consciousness detects the "little chisel/Of never-napping Time," which, when it thinks the poet sleeping, he feels "boring sly within my bones."[3]

A pair of spectacles is superimposed on all of Hardy's worlds. It is necessary to be alert to both the world viewed with remarkable insight and precision and the viewer shaping the vision. The world is watching and being watched, and the poems and novels, as they watch with loving and longing attention, strain to achieve an awareness that will protect against the watchers. In vain, of course. The self-conscious poet cannot stop, though he can detect the "boring." Seeing, which can make the world perhaps deceptively attractive, becomes a defense in that it allows the observer to anticipate the worst, to know at the very height of passion that the passion is temporary. Being observant of an observant world means being alert to the dangers of unselfconscious lapsing into touch: a class-bound culture will have its revenge; the joys of sexuality have a very short life.

II

Given the centrality of questions of perception – how and when we see what we see in Hardy's novels – it will be useful to look at Hardy's novelistic career as if it were framed by two window scenes. Each, eerily beautiful in its dark way, embodies the paradox that haunts so much of Hardy's writing: it is impossible, merely seeing, to affect what is observed, but what is observed, given humans' anomalous powers of sensibility and consciousness, has power to wound. Both scenes suggest the pervasive defensiveness of Hardy's writing strategies, his alertness to the dangers of the world he all too keenly perceives, but also his characteristic attention to the doings of a world that is often glimpsed out of the corner of one's eye, or by chance, and that is nevertheless beautiful as it goes on its indifferent way.

The first of these, breathtaking in its casual violation of what seems like a pleasant afternoon's entertainment in the Town Hall, describes Cytherea Graye's "glance" out the window and her almost surreal observation of her father's fall to his death (*DR*, ch. 1, p. 9); the second records Jude's deathbed observation of the crowds in the Christminster streets and then, while he lies dead by the side of the window, the sounds through the window of the cheers of the young men as "the doctors of the Theatre" confer "honorary degrees on the Duke of Hamptonshire and a lot more illustrious guests of that sort" (*JO*, Pt. 6, ch. 11, p. 490).

Each of the many window scenes in the novels has its own distinctive qualities: In *A Laodicean* there is the virtual silliness of De Stancy spying on the gymnastic Paula Power; In *Tess* there is Angel Clare, touched by sexual desire, watching Tess unawares rising from sleep at a moment "when a woman's soul is more incarnate than at any other time," and spying the "red interior" of her yawning mouth "as if it had been a snake"(*TD*, ch. 27,

p. 172). *The Trumpet Major* gets its narrative impetus from the opening page in which Anne Garland watches curiously from her window the newly arrived troops from whom her lover will be chosen; *The Woodlanders* begins almost ominously with barber Percomb peering in the partly open door and spying on Marty South, preparing his rape of the lock; it virtually ends with Winterborne, in the throes of loving self-sacrifice, shivering outside the window of his cabin; *Two on a Tower* does not quite use the window, but the telescope plays a similar role as Swithin St. Cleve gazes at the heavens appalled and fascinated by the nausea-inducing vastness of the skies; In *The Mayor of Casterbridge* Farfrae, with mild curiosity, watches Henchard at the mayor's banquet and enters the mayor's life fatally through the window; in *A Pair of Blue Eyes* Knight hangs on for his life staring into fossils' eyes. And there is the wonderful window scene in *Far from the Madding Crowd* at the harvest home banquet, in which Bathsheba and then Boldwood are inside the window while Gabriel Oak sits at the same table without.

The opening window scene in *Desperate Remedies* is one of those remarkable moments that give weight even to the thinnest and most compromised of Hardy's fictions. Cytherea sees the event only by chance. In the midst of some exchange with young friends, she just happens to glance out the window, where the world, "not Cytherea," is playing itself out. Closed off from the event by the window that reveals it, Cytherea sees men on a high scaffolding seeming "little larger than pigeons," as they make "their tiny movements with a soft, spirit-like silentness." We experience the moment only as Cytherea sees and hears it. When her father turns his attention to "a new stone they were lifting," Cytherea begins to register alarm: "'Why does he stand like that?' the young lady thought at length – up to that moment as listless and careless as one of the ancient Tarentines, who, on such an afternoon as this, watched from the Theatre the entry into their Harbour of a power that overturned the State" (*DR*, ch. 1, p. 10). The expansion of the casual moment to mythic proportions emphasizes the way in which forces beyond the individual consciousness enter and overturn the ordinary and taken-for-granted aspects of life. Window scenes usually activate the threat of disruption that comes from other lives we do not know or think about. Up there with her father, of course, Cytherea would have spoken in warning, but it is just the windowed distance that gives the scene its particular force. Cytherea

> unknowingly stood, as it were, upon the extreme posterior edge of a tract in her life, in which the real meaning of Taking Thought had never been

known. It was the last hour of experience she ever enjoyed with a mind entirely free from knowledge of that labyrinth in which she stepped immediately thereafter. (*DR*, ch. 1, p. 9)

Seeing reveals the world as "labyrinth." Cytherea's rite of passage to adulthood takes her to the edge of Hardy's understanding of a world that constantly surprises consciousnesses entirely bent on their own purposes. The world observable through the window is a world full of other forms of life, any one of which might impinge on one's own. Such surprises inherent in observation justify the arbitrariness that is notoriously characteristic of Hardy's world. Like so many of Hardy's characters, Cytherea "unknowingly stood."

Hardy (and his narrator) is fascinated by that condition of unknowing that precedes self-consciousness. He observes innocence that does not know it is being observed. But the fall from innocence here is without traditional moral implications of intention and complicity. While the scene describes a literal fall to death, it is more interested in the almost accidental perception of that fall and the difference between the precise casualness of the description and the fall's effects on the watching Cytherea. It is mere chance that puts her in the position of observer, and as the awareness of what is happening enters hers and the readers' consciousness she is too far away even to shout – she can do nothing about what she sees. Cytherea falls into knowledge, particularly of her own vulnerability to forces over which she can have no control and for which she is not responsible. It is certainly no accident that the fall is accompanied by a fall in social position, and henceforward it will be impossible for Cytherea ever to be unselfconscious about being observed, or about her class status.

The sequence is reported as it appears to Cytherea's consciousness, but what emerges is not registered with Jamesian complexity. There is only an initial odd sense of detachment, as though nothing great were at stake. Then, the slightest indication of unease: "'Why does he stand like that?' the young lady thought at length." Then she moves "uneasily": "I wish he would come down," she whispered, "it is so dangerous to be absent-minded up there." The power of the episode derives partly from its refusal to explore and dramatize consciousness even as it so rigorously adheres to Cytherea's point of view. But Hardy's refusal to explore consciousness in what would become the modernist way is in itself a reflection on the nature and importance of consciousness. There is no transition from the normality of a young girl's afternoon to the catastrophe; catastrophe simply, casually, happens. One kind of world suddenly impinges on another. Just before the fall, the narrator pauses to talk about how Cytherea responds physically to emotion and thought: her eyes "possessed the affectionate and liquid sparkle of loyalty and good faith," they sparkle "during pleasant doubt." She gives an involuntary "minute start" and exerts "ecstatic pressure" on the listener's arm when she tells a secret. Every gesture recorded suggests an observer who sees more than Cytherea means to tell about herself. Every gesture reveals a Cytherea unwary, innocent, and peculiarly vulnerable to the detective eye. The narrator observes Cytherea with a calculated minuteness and particularity altogether distinct from the nature of her own observations as she "glances" out the window from the theater of the local entertainment she is attending. The interest in observing her observing not only emphasizes her vulnerability by specific reference to her unpreparedness, but it dramatizes that vulnerability by the narrative self-consciousness of its own minute watching. The narrator who sees is aware of the potential price of seeing; Cytherea, the observer, is not. There is always another impinging world visible to a chance glance, or out of the corner of one's eye. For that complexity of worlds, Hardy does not turn to elaborate explorations of the protagonist's mind, but to a distant keen-eyed narrator who makes the objectively recorded visible world a labyrinth of meanings whose interpretation and even existence depends on consciousness – in this and most Hardyan cases, the narrator's.

It is characteristic of Hardy at his best that this carefully rendered moment has a quality of beautiful magic about its almost casual precision: nothing could more forcefully render the terrible oddness of powerlessness before the keenly observed. Cytherea's father, an architect, standing unselfconsciously on the scaffolding of a church spire with four workmen to whom he is giving directions,

> indecisively laid hold of one of the scaffolding-poles, as if to test its strength, then let it go and stepped back. In stepping, his foot slipped. An instant of doubling forward and sideways and he reeled off into the air immediately disappearing downwards. (ch. 1, p. 11)

Everything goes on in silence, and the prose diverts from what Cytherea cannot see to where Cytherea stands and would revert to sound except that Cytherea "gasped for breath. She could utter no sound." Sound comes from the audience among which she sits. "One by one the people about her, unconscious of what had happened, turned their heads, and inquiry and alarm became visible on their faces at the sight of the poor child. A moment longer, and she fell to the floor" with a casualness that magnifies the horror of the moment. The audience too are observed observers, upon whom the seen event impinges incongruously.

While the observer from the window cannot affect the event, the event, as virtually all of Hardy's protagonists discover, can affect her. What happens to Cytherea is nicely representative of the fate of many of Hardy's characters, whose lives turn out to spin around what enters visually, through the window. Such seeing is immediately connected with a feeling of vulnerability or, in other cases, with fear of exposure. The window moment precipitates a crisis of class and shame, in effect here revealing the social system upon which the life of Cytherea, in this way representative of Hardy's later heroines, was unselfconsciously built. *Desperate Remedies* establishes a fundamental pattern for Hardy's original sin that so many have to hide – the sin of class origins. Stephen Smith, Ethelberta, Edward Springrove, Swithin St. Cleve, George Somerset, Christopher Julian, Michael Henchard, Giles Winterborne, Clym Yeobright, and Jude Fawley – almost all of Hardy's male protagonists and some of the women – live on the cusp of their class, and their fates are entirely bound up with their power to climb, or their bad luck in falling. In effect, Cytherea is cast out of her community and her class by the fall of her father. Members of the community stare at her "with a stare unmitigated by any of the respect that had formerly softened it" (ch. 1, p. 15). *Desperate Remedies*, then, begins with the fear that dominates, to Lawrence's chagrin, all of Hardy's books and most of his central characters: the fear of being an object of "staring," that is, of being shamed by losing social position and class status. That fear almost invariably is embodied through the choral figures in the community, who have traditionally been seen as one of the peculiar sources of Hardy's charm. Formally and thematically essential to the narratives, they are ubiquitous observers who satisfy the narrative compulsion to frame all actions through distanced observation, and even more fundamentally, they are the bearers of the conventions of class and hierarchy. To avoid the shame of being observed by the community, Hardy's protagonists are driven to their often apparently mad attempts at evasion, hopeless and frustrated and inevitably observed secret elopements, disguises, and pursuits of Hardyesque melodrama. Such figures shape the careers of characters like Henchard (whose fall is precipitated by the furmity woman's public exposure of him) and, in particular, of Hardy's female protagonists.

Hardy's hypersensitivity to the possibility of being shamed is made explicit from the start in *Desperate Remedies*. Its importance to his whole canon could barely have been guessed at the time, but it provides a clue to all that followed:

> Now it is a noticeable fact that we do not much mind what men think of us, or what humiliating secret they discover of our means, parentage, or object, provided that each thinks and acts thereupon in isolation. It is the exchange of ideas about us that we dread most; and the possession by a hundred acquaintances, severally insulated, of the knowledge of our skeleton closet's whereabouts is not so distressing to the nerves as a chat over it by a party of half-a-dozen – exclusive depositaries though they may be. (ch. 1, p. 15)

The Lawrentian aspect of Hardy's art drives his protagonists into the risky worlds of natural desire; what Lawrence didn't like about Hardy is his unwillingness to be chattered about by "a party of half-a-dozen." For Hardy, it is not so much the sin or the crime that disturbs as the possibility that two or more of the community may be talking about us without our knowledge, sharing stories, true or false, of our wrongdoings. Here is where one can recognize the persistent difference in Hardy between guilt and shame, and in this distinction the "window" plays a crucial role. It is not what is going on that matters as much as how it is perceived, and by whom.

For a character like Tess, however, shame and guilt entangle; Tess bears the burdens of her culture and feels the guilt that Hardy writes to condemn. As I have already suggested, the imposition of social convention on the "natural" constitutes one of the major crimes in Hardy's world. Tess internalizes the judgments of society, as they will be enacted by Angel later in the novel. But Tess has not sinned and should not feel guilty. In describing Tess after her encounter with Alex, the narrator contrasts her sense of guilt with her extraordinary and beautiful harmony with "the element she moved in." "Walking among the sleeping birds in the hedges, watching the skipping rabbits on a moonlit warren, or standing under a pheasant-laden bough, she looked upon herself as a figure of Guilt intruding into the haunts of innocents" (ch. 13, p. 91). Here is a characteristic moment of Hardy's greatest art, in which the drama or melodrama is set in the context of the living world beyond the protagonist. Tess, although otherwise in harmony with "the element she moved in," brings human guilt into the haunts of those rabbits and pheasants whose unknowing, innocent lives go on regardless of her drama, and regardless of the constraints of social norms. This habit of Hardy's of reminding readers of the lives of nonhuman others – not only pheasants and rabbits and birds but ants and moths and slugs – gives to his nervously defensive and gloomy art a vitality, a sense of the value of life, that resists his own shame and the shame at being ashamed that so often structures his plots. The juxtapositions are never merely ornamental, but intimations of another kind of narrative that is essential to the nature of Lawrentian life. Tess is no more guilty than the pheasants or the rabbits. The true guilt belongs to those who are shamed by their acquiescence in arbitrary "shreds of convention."

Hardy himself, however, is one of those. There is a lightly comic but moving sequence in *The Hand of Ethelberta*, in which that kind of guilt is dramatized. Ethelberta tries to keep secret from a group of wealthy aristocrats that she could only afford to travel to a meeting on an aged overworked ass that she rents for three shillings. The ass is discovered by the group, who wonder how it got there, and Ethelberta professes absolute ignorance. " 'Many come and picnic here,'" she said serenely, "and the animal may have been left till they return from some walk." Lord Montclere ignorantly responds, "True." Animals, do their work here: "The humble ass hung his head in his usual manner and it demanded little fancy from Ethelberta to imagine that he despised her." Ethelberta is ashamed of her behavior, which implies as well that she is ashamed of her family and her father – a butler, whom she imagines is at that moment working in an underground pantry. "With a groan at her inconsistency in being ashamed of the ass . . . [Ethelberta] said in her heart, 'My God, what a thing am I!'" (*HE*, ch. 31, p. 249). Guilty because she is ashamed, she enacts Hardy's own guilt.

In spite of himself, Hardy is bound by the very conventions and social discriminations, the very arbitrariness of class distinctions and hierarchies, that all of his hidden energies are driven to expose and denigrate. His concern about writing for money is articulated in *A Pair of Blue Eyes* by Harry Knight, who tells Elfride, "It requires judicious omission of your real thoughts to make a novel popular" (*PBE*, ch. 17, p. 186). His sensitivity to observation is exacerbated by his fears not only that his real thoughts will be detected but that he has compromised himself. The complex publishing history of *Tess*, Hardy's acquiescence in bowdlerization for serial publication and its further revisions through the 1890s until a final form was achieved in 1912 for the Wessex edition, reveals willingness to compromise for the sake of respectability and money. Hardy seems to have felt both ashamed and guilty for being so.

The hand of guilty Ethelberta hangs darkly over much of Hardy's fiction. His characters are often not disturbed by the fact of their transgressions, while invariably they are almost overwhelmed by the possibility that these will become public matter. He invents grotesquely implausible plots that place his characters in technical jeopardy without compromising their innocence, but then has them act as though the technical transgression constitutes a deep moral violation. Cytherea feels compromised because there are rumors suggesting that she consummated her marriage with Manston after the (false) information is spread that his wife might still be alive. No actual bigamy occurs in the novel. Lady Constantine behaves similarly in *Two on a Tower*, and Elfride's kiss of Stephen Smith is sufficient to destroy her life. These extravagances anticipate Tess's fate and Sue Bridehead's convincing and maddening "modern" neurosis. In every case, the crime is not in the commission but in the power of social shame to provoke guilt among the innocent. In all of these cases, questions of sexuality, guilt, and shame are bound into questions of social hierarchy and respectability.

Sexual energy, which the protagonists of almost all of the novels struggle to contain and disguise, is a danger here. There is, as with Tess, very little sign that the novels endorse the shame the protagonists, particularly the women, feel when this energy is aroused – crossing classes and disrupting the lives of everyone from Boldwood to Jude, from Bathsheba to Tess. Sex becomes a great leveler, guaranteeing exposure of the arbitrariness of class distinction. But the true crime is not desire; it is guilt for being unwilling to honor it – the guilt, for example, of Angel Clare.

Hardy is, as in all matters, strongly ambivalent about the ideal if not about destructive idealists like Clare. The ideal is a persistent motif in Hardy, and his fiction-writing career climaxes with a direct exploration and questioning of it in the strange experimental *The Well-Beloved*. In that novel, which I will be discussing fully in a later chapter, the protagonist, the sculptor, Jocelyn Pierston, pursues through three generations an ideal lover who is always inaccessible in the flesh. While Jocelyn's ideal is an active creative force, it is also represented with an almost comic irony as absurdly out of touch with the texture of human life. Jocelyn sees himself, as Hardy viewed himself, as something of a child. In *The Hand of Ethelberta*, Christopher Julian, another artist-figure protagonist, who is in love with Ethelberta, is described by his sister: "I should say you were a child in your impulses, and an old man in your reflections" (ch. 11, p. 89). Idealists, belying the sheer materiality of desire, end up murderers: the ideally named Knight (*A Pair of Blue Eyes*) and Angel Clare (*Tess of the D'Urbervilles*) are responsible for the deaths of Elfride Swancourt and Tess herself. Angel tells Tess (as Jocelyn was to feel about his beloved ones) that "the woman I have been loving is not you," but "another woman in your shape" (ch. 35, p. 226). It is one of the major and most moving concerns of Hardy's novels that the ideal and the natural world come into radical conflict. When the ideal wins out there are painful material consequences. Nature, so cruel or indifferent in so many of Hardy's novels, emerges instead in understory as innocent and beautiful.

The quest for the ideal that characterizes so many of Hardy's plots runs counter to the time-bound character of the physical that the prose celebrates. Hardy's métier is the frustration plot, which dramatizes the cost of idealizing love. The alternative to the ideal is a radical acceptance of the utter materiality of life, something that is almost parodied in the prematurely old little Father Time, in *Jude*, who almost laughably articulates that view: "I should like the flowers very much," he says, "if I didn't keep on thinking they'd be all withered in a few days" (pt. 5, ch. 5, p. 366). In extremes of youthful passion Hardy's characters are beset with premonitions of fading flesh and dying romance. The neurasthenic sensitivity to time is a reflex of irrepressible desire.

Hardy's deepest sympathies are, as Lawrence and Woolf believed, with the natural energies of life, nonhuman and human, with intensities of sexual passion which shame him, with the recklessness and excesses that his prose never allows one to forget, and that, Lawrence complains, his stories invariably punish through the forces of shame and convention. Sexual passion is particularly dangerous because intense youthful feelings will dissipate inside the enforced rituals of respectability, that is, marriage. The moment becomes the lifetime, with usually awful results. Just as Henchard's irrational ambivalent energies for both restraint and ambition mark him as doomed and irresistibly attractive as novelistic subject, so Tess's sexuality is honored by the text that kills her for it. (Is she lucky to die before, in their marriage, their passion would have died?) Both move through their novels on the edge of advanced social standing; both, but particularly Tess, are trapped in the energies of sexuality. But for each, the primary narrative question has to do with class. Henchard, the migrant farm worker, becomes mayor; Tess, the peasant girl, marries a clergyman's son. Their dignity is in the integrity of their "crimes," their power both to internalize and stand against the forces that will condemn them. When Tess finally succumbs to her passion for Angel, the narrative comments:

> In reality she was drifting into acquiescence. Every see-saw of her breath, every wave of her blood, every pulse singing in her ears, was a voice that joined with nature in revolt against her scrupulousness. Reckless, inconsiderate acceptance of him; to close with him at the altar, revealing nothing, and chancing discovery; to snatch ripe pleasure before the iron teeth of pain could have time to shut upon her; that was what love counseled; and in almost a terror of ecstasy Tess divined that, despite her many months of

lonely self-chastisement, wrestlings, communings, schemes to lead a future
of austere isolation, love's counsel would prevail. (ch. 28, p. 179)

Although nature is in revolt against her scrupulousness, Tess bears in her
consciousness the narrator's imagination of the consequences of passion,
even in the midst of passion. The disparity between "natural" law and
human conventions dooms any reckless acquiescence in the natural. It is
not only Tess's desire that drives the narrative; it is the desire of the narrator
who knows too much. There is no guilt in Tess's ultimate acquiescence,
but there is the inevitability of shame and the imposition upon her of
society's demand that there should be guilt. In the end, Hardy characteristically reestablishes the perspective of distance and disengagement, where
society imposes its violent punishment. The moments of violence – the
deaths of Alec and of Tess – are not seen, but presented through strategies
of visual distancing: the widening red spot on the ceiling observed by the
landlady, the remote prospect of the black flag that Angel and Liza-Lu
observe from the top of the Great West Hill, looking back at the town and
the octagonal tower where Tess is executed. Such distancing is crucial here
because Angel and Liza-Lu represent another violation of the categories of
class that proved so expensive for Tess.

Hardy's revulsion from and ambivalence about the arbitrariness of class
hierarchy is built into almost every novel, as characters cross the boundaries
or are through bad luck dropped from the aristocracy to the agrarian poor,
or by hard work and discipline (necessary always with a trace of luck) raised
into the middle class. In *A Laodicean*, Paula Power occupies the De Stancy
mansion, bought by her rich industrialist father, and is almost corrupted by
the attractions of the class she has dispossessed. In *Two on a Tower* Lady
Constantine falls in love with Swithin, who is not only several years her
junior, but whose parents work menially on her estate. In *A Pair of Blue
Eyes* Stephen Smith is first accepted as Elfride's lover because he is thought
to be of good family and then rejected because his father is a "rural
mechanic," although actually wealthier than Elfride's father.

Hiding and secrecy and exposure are therefore central to Hardy's plots,
and even those who are wary of being observed end by being observed from
an unexpected quarter. It is difficult not to return to the almost parodic
parade of spying in *Desperate Remedies*. Each of the observers, except the
professional detective, has a large stake in preserving a dishonorable secret
that will sustain his or her position in society. Anne Seaway, rightly afraid
for her life, observes the villainous and beautiful Manston (who, acciden-
tally observing himself in the mirror, is precipitated into action). Carefully

concealed from observation, she follows him to a room where he has hidden the body of his true wife, whose place Anne is falsely taking; then Anne tries to flee, only to discover that there is another observer of Manston's hiding there, a detective. She follows the as-yet-unidentified detective, who follows Manston, who is bearing the body of his wife. Anne then discovers that the man she is following is being followed by another woman (who, it develops, is Cytherea Aldclyffe): "intentness pervaded everything; Night herself seemed to have become a watcher" (ch. 19, p. 350).

Night in Hardy is indeed "a watcher." But so too is Day. Everyone has something to hide; everyone will be exposed: Miss Aldclyffe is discovered; Manston's secret is revealed; the detective is himself caught and knocked out; Anne's participation in Manston's conspiracy is made clear to the detective. This mad and melodramatic scene is, in the end, only an exaggerated and melodramatic enactment of Hardy's persistent concerns in novel after novel. His plots and his own life are constrained and shaped by his continuing fear of exposure. Here again, great knowledge accompanies disaster. Extravagant as this first instance of multiple spying is, there are many, almost as absurd, throughout Hardy's later work. Whether internally or externally, the judgment of the community is embedded in the revelations of observation, and these determine the directions of Hardy's narratives, as they turn compulsively to questions of guilt, respectability, and class.

They return famously again, in *Jude the Obscure*, where gloom dominates as visions of the ambient living world of understory diminish. Distanced seeing initiates the narrative: Jude first sees the distant Christminster as a cluster of remote shining spots, then as "a halo or glow-fog" (Bk 1, ch. 3, p. 63). The imagination of Christminster, especially as the home of his former teacher, Phillotson, inspires Jude to dreams of living the university life that goes with it. The dream of 5,000 pounds a year (4,500 for charity!) once again connects vision with questions of class.

But *Jude* is not so intensely preoccupied with watching and spying as is *Desperate Remedies*. Nor does the narrator, with Hardy's usual gorgeous and moving concentration, focus on the visible world as a kind of speaking image, like the insects on Tess's white gown, or the marks of social discrimination, as in *Far from the Madding Crowd*, where the narrator notes the identifying signs of different agricultural laborers seeking employment: "Carters and wagoners were distinguished by having a piece of whip-cord twisted around their hats; thatchers wore a fragment of woven straw; shepherds held their sheepcrooks in their hands" (ch. 6, p. 35) or those innumerable seemingly gratuitous moments in many of the novels when the narrator's eye turns toward insects or snails or animals and birds.

But while Jude is barely visible himself to the dons and scholars of the city, the novel moves from distant seeing to touching, from an attempt to establish the position of unobserved observer to a frank confrontation with the consequences of physical rather than visual engagement – from scholarship to the working class. Before the final window scenes, there are several other important ones: these are not given to protected seeing, unobserved or observing, or even to Cytherea's sort of vision of her falling father. They are, rather, passages from vision to touch. Both Jude and Sue, through different windows, hear the scream of a trapped rabbit. Jude moves from window to door in order to put the rabbit out of its agony. But they lead him to Sue's window, where she, ready to respond in the same way and aware of Jude's sensibilities, half expects him. As they speak through the window, "she let go of the casement-stay and put her hand upon his, her moonlit face regarding him wistfully." Jude kisses her hand, and, at the close of the interview, "in a moment of impulse," Sue

> bent over the sill, and laid her face upon his hair, weeping, and imprinting a scarcely perceptible little kiss upon the top of his head, withdrawing quickly so that he could not put his arms around her. (Bk 4, ch. 2, p. 277)

The window, in the end, serves to protect from consummation, but the yielding to impulse, a deadly act in Hardy's fiction, has already violated the strategies of distanced perception that Hardy and his characters consistently use elsewhere.

More extravagantly, the window is the scene of Sue's fullest expression of her revulsion from touch. Instinctively, when Phillotson unselfconsciously enters the bedroom where he and his first wife had slept but where Sue, refusing to be touched, now sleeps, she springs from the bed, "mounted upon the sill and leapt out." The impervious screen of the window is penetrated in *Jude*. The window, rather than a place of self-conscious observation, becomes a place of unselfconscious yielding to impulse. *Jude* risks violating distance and shattering the barriers of class and the conventions of sexual respectability. The consequence is, in a way, played out in Sue's last scene with Phillotson – perhaps the climax in Hardy's work of his exploration of the consequence of failing to maintain distance – when she begs him to let her cross the threshold to his room. Phillotson leads her through the doorway, and "lifting her bodily, kissed her. A quick look of aversion passed over her face, but clenching her teeth she uttered no cry" (Bk 6, ch. 9, p. 479).

Horrifying as this is, the horror of public judgment, as it is discussed by the narrator of *Desperate Remedies*, remains powerful, shaping Sue's curious career and Jude's as well. After their abortive attempt to marry, Jude and Sue find the grocer's boy no longer tips his hat to them, and they are encircled with "an oppressive atmosphere"; the communal rejection finally extends to Jude's work. Jude and Sue cannot escape observation – "I had no idea," says Jude, "that anybody was going intrude into such a lonely place and see us." They come to understand that they have lived in "a fool's paradise of supposed unrecognition" (Bk 5, ch. 6, p. 375). They are being observed after all. Here, *Jude* brings to a climax Hardy's obsession with observation: distraught at Father Time's suicide and the killing of her children, Sue hears "two persons in conversation somewhere without"; "They are talking about us, no doubt!" moaned Sue. Falling back on the language of the New Testament, "We are made a spectacle unto the world, and to angels, and to men!" (Bk 6, ch. 3, p. 417). It is, ironically, this shamed assumption of being observed that leads her back to Phillotson and his repulsive but respectable touch.

Even the invisible are observed in Hardy's world, and even this novel deliberately withdrawn from the extraordinary, if painful, pleasures of Hardyesque observation of the natural world depends upon a recognition that everything is watched and judged. But the window that is central to the last moments of Hardy's career as a novelist, as it is to Jude's last moments, is not the sort of medium of distanced observation that it would have been in earlier novels. This is no scene of a fall like Cytherea's from innocence to knowledge. Rather, the scene begins with Jude already a fallen figure, almost without the powers of perception, who has never succeeded in rising above his class, who is at least a quasi-alcoholic, and whose sexual energies have been almost equally thwarted. Having lived in a fool's paradise of social invisibility, Jude, dying, becomes almost literally invisible – and blind. When he calls out for "a little water" in the room that Arabella has abandoned in answering the seductive call of the sounds of music and celebration that drift through the window, nobody can hear him. He is too ill to see out. In effect, while the narrator's eye ironically juxtaposes the inside and the outside, Jude is both blind and invisible. As he whispers the bleak verses from Job – "Let the day perish wherein I was born" – the voices from outside are counterpointed, cheering the Remembrance games with their "Hurrah." Jude's death is unwatched and yet cheered (Bk 6, ch. 11, p. 486).

What enters Jude's consciousness through the window marks a last irony in a life that has failed to be respectable. The scene is Hardy's final exploration of the strange complex of vision, class, and sex that is central to his entire narrative oeuvre. The scene, in which vision fails, can be taken as a critique of the strategies of distanced, unobserved seeing that provoke Hardy's characters to shame and guilt in their quests both to protect themselves and to indulge their dangerous ambitions. Arabella survives by leaving the window and self-consciousness; Sue crosses the threshold to touching in a desperate recuperation of propriety; Jude becomes invisible while the outside world retains its power to wound.

By forgoing his strategies of distanced and protected observation in *Jude the Obscure*, Hardy makes it clear why they are so important to him as a novelist. *Jude* is Hardy's most disturbing, if not his most satisfying, book for several reasons. First, as I have argued, it does not for the most part intrude an understory to provide the consolations of the visible world that so movingly enrich almost every one of his other novels, no matter how bleak their implications might be. It is difficult to find in *Jude* what Gillian Beer rightly finds in most of Hardy's work – "a sense of plenitude, an appetite for joy." Second, it forgoes the protection of distanced viewing. While the narrator's voice occasionally sagely and gloomily endorses a dark vision of modern civilization, most of such commentary is given to the characters themselves. There are few moments of visionary respite or protection as windows become permeable and touch replaces sight as the dominant, impelling narrative sense. Third, in *Jude* the fantasy of aspiration beyond the limits of the working class is entirely thwarted. Ironically, although one would imagine such thwarting is characteristic of all of Hardy's writing, his novels tend to reflect a vision of a mobile society in which, from one generation to the next, a Stephen Smith or a George Somerset or an Egbert Mayne might lift himself by professional and intellectual effort into the middle class. The comedy of *The Hand of Ethelberta* actually sustains Ethelberta's attempt to move into the aristocracy from a working-class family. In *Tess*, Liza-Lu does end with Angel Clare. But in *Jude* the working class is invisible. Each figure is locked inside a conventional and repressive social system. And finally, sexuality, always dangerous in Hardy though always attractive, becomes thoroughly repulsive. Arabella's exuberant sexuality, perhaps the one instance of joyful touching in the book, insistently impedes the fragile and neurotic love of Sue and Jude and any possibility of Jude's advancement.

Finally, then, *Jude* rejects seeing as the narrative impulse of Hardy's writing. The daring of the novel's engagement with the modern and with his own career exposes Hardy to the sorts of critiques that, he imagines here, might well have thwarted his ambitions, his urgent need to remain unobserved and respectable. The visionary, the emphasis on seeing, diminishes as Hardy confronts the consequences of touching and engage-ment: *Jude* becomes a powerfully antivisionary narrative, not quite the full conclusion of his novel-writing career. The extensive exploration of the ideal in *The Well-Beloved* provides its conclusive complement. Neither book will indulge the very special quality of much of his previous work – the deep insight into an implicit reverence for the abundance, vitality, and unsuspected beauty of the natural world. This latter quality, ominously missing from *Jude*, marks the Hardy I am seeking in this book.

CHAPTER 2

Hardy and Darwin
An Enchanting Hardy?

That Hardy is really not hard to find. The understory of so many of his novels leads to what might be felt as an almost enchanted (or mysteriously disenchanted) vision. When Hardy's prose turns to what might seem mere natural description, it has an extraordinary literal persuasiveness that issues out in a strong feeling for the uncanny complexities of nature. Although *Jude the Obscure* largely avoids such moments, Jude is introduced to the reader as a figure who is torn by the recognition that there is always an understory and that life is not all about humans, their needs, and desires. Impractical but admirable, Jude feels the force of the claims of the crows he has been employed to keep away from the farmer's fields. The novel, then, takes the division between the outward drama and the reality of the understory as a given, to focus all of its energies on ways that humans have constructed culture to ignore how nature really works and thus, on the whole, have made life more difficult than it needs to be. *Jude* struggles with this tension but does not intimate the kind of vitality that can redeem Hardy's stories from their life-denying energies. They almost always include moments of enchantment that follow from Hardy's intense attention to how nature works: Hardy's novels teach us to see beyond the immediate moment, the immediate place, to achieve a kind of Darwinian understanding of how nature works, and how the immediate object of our vision is part of a vast complex of connections in both space and time. Such a recognition can itself be uncomfortable, but it is also, for his characters, a condition for coming to terms with the relentlessness of natural selection – those best adapted to their place are most likely to survive. In Hardy, this law is complicated enormously by culture, yet his narrators almost always manage to reveal a world that evokes the wonder that Darwin himself regularly evoked in his prose.[1]

On the way to a consideration of the aspects of Hardy's art that resist the darkness of his overall vision, I have so far focused on a clash of preoccupations, primarily the tension between sexual energy and social norms, that predictably issue in disasters for protagonists. But I have tried also to suggest how, counterpointed to these human dramas, Hardy regularly implies an understory, dramas beyond the human, vital forces, most often unperceived by the protagonists, that affirm the life the dramas themselves seem to deny. Penny Boumelha summarizes what she takes to be a critical consensus about Hardy in this way: "there resides within Hardy's realism a significant presence of something more like a texture or a rhythm than a narrative impulsion."[2] These give a distinctive quality to Hardy's overt pessimism and a delicate beauty to his art. Before proceeding, then, with consideration of particular novels and passages in which such forces are manifest, it will be useful to turn attention briefly to the inescapable Darwin, whose own prose so regularly contradicts the dark interpretation of them that always gives the word "Darwinian" an ominous quality. Obviously a critically important figure in Hardy's thought and imagination, Darwin is normally associated with the dark side – "O why should Nature's law be mutual butchery!" (Bk 5, ch. 6, p. 378) cries Sue.

But if Darwin's arguments make Hardy confront that "butchery" unblinkered, they also intensify awareness of the complex ways in which nature works and of our mutual dependence on other forms of life, on their abundance, richness, and beauty, and, equally important, on their individuality. The sensibility that produces Hardyan enchantment is still visible in Jude's sudden recognition of the claims of the crows, or his compassion for the dying rabbit, or his horrified slaughter of the pig. Jude might be taken as a naïve Hardy, with instinctive compassion for all living things, where they all must participate in a "struggle for existence." It perhaps does not help one's own survival to recognize the claims of others involved in that struggle, but the understory of Hardy's novels almost invariably forces that recognition, and the awareness that we all matter equally. We are all, as Darwin argues near the end of *On the Origin of Species*, quite literally one family. Once the theory of evolution by natural selection is accepted, Darwin claims,

> The terms used by naturalists of affinity, relationship, community of type, paternity, morphology, adaptive characters, rudimentary and aborted organs, &c. will cease to be metaphorical, and will have a plain signification. (*OS*, p. 485)

These are not analogies; they are homologies. They are literal. Relationships are literal; paternity is literal. Those organs really are "aborted," incomplete development of complete organs in earlier forms. For Darwin implicitly, and for Hardy explicitly, this fact changes humans' relation to the rest of the natural world.

In a frequently cited passage of a letter written to the secretary of the Humanitarian League in 1910, Hardy wrote:

> Few people seem to perceive fully as yet that the most far reaching conse-
> quence of the establishment of the common origin of all species is ethical:
> that it logically involved a re-adjustment of altruistic morals by enlarging as
> a *necessity of rightness* the application of what has been called "The Golden
> Rule" beyond the area of mankind to that of the whole animal kingdom.
> (*LWTH*, pp. 376–377)

When considering the importance of Darwin to Hardy, then, one needs to recognize that the inevitable catching of Darwinian strains in Hardy just where there is stress, competition, chance, struggle, and suffering is more than a little unbalanced. Darwin hovers everywhere in Hardy's worlds: he is there in the fossil eyes into which Henry Knight stares as he clings for his life to the side of the cliff in *A Pair of Blue Eyes*; we hear him again as the trees rub against each other in the crowded forest of *The Woodlanders*; and again in the squealing of the trapped rabbit. But we should be hearing him as well in Hardy's prose that catches the sound of the wind in the trees, or Giles Winterborne's almost magical capacity to make things grow, or Tess's unselfconscious sensuousness. There can be no doubt that Hardy found in Darwin exactly what he claims – grounds for expansion of the Golden Rule – and much more, perhaps less obvious but certainly as fundamental.

A. Dwight Culler was right many years ago when he wrote that "to trace the way in which ... writers derive from Darwin their views of nature, man, God, and society does not ... quite get at the heart of the problem."[3] It is, says Culler, the *form* of Darwin's argument that counts most. Culler meant, in particular, the form of paradox and irony, instrumental in expressing Darwin's reversal of natural theology, explaining adaptation as the creation not of a guiding intelligence but of "chance" (although Darwin did not believe in chance).[4] I want to amend Culler's important suggestion that we must pay attention to the way Darwin wrote by insisting that we must also attend to the kinds of moral inferences Hardy drew from Darwin's way of seeing. Darwin himself, as we know, read nature with moral judgment, and recoiled in horror from some of its nastiest practices. Personally and publicly, he had to find a way to make his researches compatible with Christian morality, and as a scientist, he was obliged to make simple description his primary work, though it was description always more or less surreptitiously supported by hypotheses and cultural leanings. So it is in Darwin's *way* of writing that one comes to recognize his way of *feeling* about what he describes, and it is easy to detect in his minute attention to even the minutest phenomena a curiosity that extends into something like enchantment. Darwin looks patiently long and hard at natural phenomena and he finds in them not only the experience of wonder, but vestiges of deep history and complex interconnection. There is a marvelous anecdote about him recorded in Janet Browne's biography of Darwin. When asked about Darwin's health, his gardener replied,

> my poor master has been very sadly. I often wish he had something to do. He moons about in the garden, and I have seen him stand doing nothing before a flower for ten minutes at a time. If he only had something to do I really believe he would be better.[5]

Rapt in the details of natural processes, Darwin sees ways beyond the limits of casual observation and finds patterns and meaning, and it is this Darwin I want to consider. The inferences from what he saw in those long moments of attention are of less importance for the Darwin in Hardy's art than the modes of attention to what might be seen. Those modes imply an engagement so intense as to suggest a loving, and ethically charged relationship with the whole range of nature, organic and inorganic. The first thing required is seeing right and then describing what is seen. These are the essential activities of both scientist and poet, and this kind of deeply caring activity is at the root of Hardy's aesthetically self-conscious and risky engagement with literary forms. Darwin's gardener, observing the staring Darwin, did not know that something really active was going on. Hardy's readers, attending quite reasonably to the dark direction his stories take, do not give adequate emphasis to that love of life manifest in his meticulous descriptions of the nonhuman world. He was more in love with life, and in Darwinian ways, than most typical Darwinian readings suggest.

I want to assert once again that through all the darkness of a chance-driven, mindless world against which thought-endowed animals like humans have to struggle hopelessly, there glimmers steadily a strong morally driven affirmation of life. Darwin's vision of the world is hardly as gloomy as most of his interpreters make it; Hardy's world implies an underlying vision of the possibilities (rarely, it is true, fulfilled) of human flourishing and fullness. Perhaps most important, it is saturated, as Beer says, with a feeling for "the whole of the animal kingdom," a feeling that is often the source of Hardy's aesthetic power. Perhaps the "happiness" that

Beer finds behind Hardy's darkness is something of a stretch, but the experience of "fullness" is there for the reading.

I will in this chapter be adopting this word out of Charles Taylor and Jane Bennett to replace Beer's "happiness."[6] Taylor describes fullness as "an experience which unsettles and breaks through our ordinary sense of being in the world, with its familiar objects, activities and points of reference." His first example of the experience is in a passage that is triggered by elements remarkably similar to passages from Hardy that I will discuss in the last chapter: "A lark rose suddenly from the ground beside the tree where I was standing and poured out its song above my head, and then sank still singing to rest. Everything then grew still as the sunset faded and the veil of dusk began to cover the earth" (Taylor, p. 5). Although the passage Taylor cites registers awe deriving from the intensified natural experience as though it were an opening to God, Hardy's parallel but rigorously naturalist passages create a similar feeling of breaking through the ordinary to a deep feeling *for* the natural world. This is what happens in Hardy's finest poetic prose, and, I would argue, implicitly in many passages in Darwin: they open to an experience of fullness and thus to a feeling for the richness of life. Such experience does not necessarily constitute "happiness," but it does imply a sense of the value and meaningfulness of the world that makes even of defeat and loss something very much worth living for.

Although in the *Origin* Darwin was obviously very much the scientist, the book is marked throughout by emotional responses and alertness to the possible emotional implications of his facts and theory. Alert to possible dark inferences, he was careful to seek consolation, sometimes unconvincingly. He claimed, in a passage that has always seemed feebly apologetic, that "we may console ourselves with the full belief that the war of nature is not incessant, that no fear is felt, that death is generally prompt, and that the vigorous, the healthy, and the happy survive and multiply" (*OS*, p. 79). And while this is hardly a formulation of fullness and is certainly insufficiently consolatory, the very quest for consolation suggests how his work is marked by a sense of the emotional implications of what he was discovering and arguing. His view that even in its crudest formulation natural selection requires a world of organisms content enough with their lives to desire to sustain and propagate them makes sense, in a tradition common to the natural theology he was self-consciously displacing. A darker reading is yet possible: even in the most miserable of lives, the pleasure of the procreative act would lead to continuation of the species.

But the sense of "breaking through" survives Darwin's more practical and less inspiring explanations. Even as the processes he describes move mercilessly and without consciousness, Darwin makes his case by looking with loving attention and wonder at the processes themselves and in so doing makes possible the sense of fullness that flourishes most richly in Hardy's prose.

While few of Hardy's characters are dramatized as achieving fullness (a word too rich and various to submit to easy definition), the novels themselves might well be experienced as intimations of that state. Taylor implies that fullness is achievable only through religious experience, and thus my transfer of the term to Darwin and Hardy would seem misguided. But the burden of my argument is that Darwin and Hardy might be seen as writers who make that transfer, who dramatize the aspiration to and the possibility of the experience of fullness within a world conceived as entirely secular. They both write in a tradition of natural history that Amy King has described as "reverent empiricism,"[7] finding in the astonishing details that the great natural historians wrote about intimations of a divine hand. The awe inspired by these details and by the scientist's, the naturalist's, the poet's meticulous registration of them stretches across religion and science. The vestige of this awe, which in Taylor's example leads back to the experience of fullness and the divine, in secular writers like Darwin and Hardy remains powerful and soul-satisfying. In the midst of describing the details of a world driven by natural selection, or in the midst of describing the scene of the death of Clym Yeobright's mother in *Return of the Native*, Hardy and Darwin image forth a world "wonderful," as Darwin says, and beautiful, as Hardy shows it to be.

The idea of fullness is connected directly to another idea central to Taylor's discussion: the idea, of "enchantment," and I consider this concept in relation to Hardy's art, largely through the focus of the ideas of Jane Bennett.

I do not want to claim that despite the tragic direction of so many of his novels, Hardy's work is specifically designed to affirm life. A Darwinian kind of thematic pessimism is easy to find in the novels, but so too is a Darwinian kind of affirmation, growing from Darwin's *way* of looking at the world, rather than from inferences from his explicit ideas. The understory of Hardy's novels, which, from the perspective of Lawrence and Woolf, gives them their greatest distinction, is built on intense and precise observation of the natural world. Readers who look past or through the plots and attend to the texture of Hardy's best prose will hear the counterpoint and recognize Hardy's own instinctive (and at the same time artful) attraction to the workings of the natural world, from which a vibrant and wonderful sense of life emerges forcefully.

An attentive reading of Darwin, noting the language he uses in constructing the concept of "natural selection," makes clear that for him the world, with all the horrors that he too uncovered, remained irresistibly attractive; a similarly attentive reading of Hardy would work the same magic. Hardy knows and repeatedly makes clear that the enchantment, the beauty, the form, the pleasures of nature are not intrinsic to it but the work of those excessive, hyperactive human nerves, which have learned to read nature and impose form on it. The effect, whether the magic is in the mind or the landscape, is enchantment. For both Darwin and Hardy, the naturalization and rationalization of the world, as Max Weber described the disenchanting effect of scientific work, did not disenchant, did not close out the possibilities of fullness, and did not exclude the possibility of a secular ethics. In my *Darwin Loves You: Natural Selection and the Re-enchantment of the World*, I try to make this case for Darwin's writing.[8] I want in this chapter to extend the argument to Hardy.

The main direction of Hardy's novels, it must be conceded, reveals Hardy subject to and struggling with a widely held Victorian (and even modern) view: when religion is lost, morality, value, hope, and fullness disappear; no secular alternative could possibly fill the void. Without some all-inclusive religious scheme, the enchantment that once (so Taylor insists) infused all aspects of one's life with spiritual significance would seem to be unattainable. Yet Hardy, perhaps the gloomiest of the early post-Darwinians, provides evidence for Bennett's view that the world does not suddenly empty of value when religion disappears. Bennett criticizes the argument that with the loss of religion and teleology, the here and now, our very material lives, come to seem without meaning, amoral, valueless. Value depends, so the argument goes, on a transcendent power: "The depiction of nature and culture as orders no long capable of inspiring deep attachment infects the self as a creature of loss and thus discourages discernment of the marvelous vitality of bodies human and nonhuman, natural and artefactual."[9] Few Victorian writers saw so clearly as Hardy "the marvelous vitality of bodies human and nonhuman"; few saw so clearly that Darwin's world is full of the spirit of place, that place has its history, its Wordsworthian memories, and that nature still has the power to evoke excitement and wonder and awe and to "inspire deep attachment."

Equally important for my purposes here is Bennett's effort to explain what enchantment really is: "To be enchanted is to be struck and shaken by the extraordinary that lives amid the familiar and the everyday" (p. 4). This might serve as a description of Hardy's Victorian romantic/realist project, and a description as well of Darwin's repeated "wonder" and awe at the ordinary ways of nature, the variety of growth in a cup of soil, the woodpecker adapting to life where there are no woods, or the extraordinary efficiency of ants and bees.

"The overall effect of enchantment," Bennett says, "is a mood of fullness, plenitude, or liveliness, a sense of having had one's nerves or circulation or concentration powers tuned up and recharged" (p. 5). I will in later chapters be reading carefully passages in which this "tune-up" and "recharging" happen – as in the first paragraph of *Under the Greenwood Tree* describing the distinguishable sounds the wind makes moving through trees, or the bird's-eye view of Casterbridge's squared-off geography, or Diggory Venn's gambling by the light of glowworms, or Gabriel Oak fighting off the storm and protecting the harvest, or Giles Winterborne disappearing into the green of the tree he is shrouding, or Tess's crawling hunt through the mead in search of tiny shoots of garlic. The almost paranoid quality of so many of Hardy's narratives, in which, even in the remotest places, no secret ever remains secret, also creates a world in which everything matters, everything means. The world is alive with what each of us at the moment does not see but that the narrator does see. Everywhere in Hardy, even when the effects are unhappy, there are objects and actions that spur life and awareness. Hardy's work recognizes universal connectedness – both material and moral – and takes the realist ideal of attributing to the "ordinary" the values appropriate to tragedy and epic to levels that reach beyond realism to something like "fullness."

Darwin, of course, does this from the start, in his discussion in his chapter on "The Struggle for Existence," of the way "plants and animals, more remote in the scale of nature, are bound together by a web of complex relations" (p. 73). In one area "Cattle absolutely determine the existence of Scotch fir" (p. 72), in another "a certain fly" and the birds that eat it, themselves regulated by predators, determine whether cattle and horses would "become feral," which in its turn would determine the nature of the vegetation, which would in turn affect the fly (p. 73). It is a wild circle of interconnection where everything matters to everything else; there is nothing unimportant in these landscapes. Darwin's last book on Vegetable Mold demonstrates how the whole of England's green and pleasant land is dependent on worm defecation! The work of careful observation, even of worm defecation, produces a shock of invigoration and excitement.

Bennett's sense of enchantment is particularly relevant to Hardy's because it is experienced inside a world that has lost both god and teleology while remaining morally significant and sustaining. Hardy's world is, quite literally, *wonder*ful, even if the wonder is often evoked (as in the heavens that Swithin and Lady Constantine observe through a telescope) by what Max Weber would have called "calculable" forces, that is, forces explicable rationally, by scientific investigation.[10] There is no avoiding the shiver of wonder and excitement as they recognize in the vast depths of the heavens the infinitesimal smallness of their own lives, but in the novel sublime astronomy becomes a kind of human lovemaking. At every point in Hardy's world one is forced into recognitions of connection and into an awareness of the importance of the small even to the sublime.

The world Bennett describes is not "purposive," nor is it "meaningful" in the way religious experience makes life meaningful, connecting our individual lifetimes with the divine and permanent. Its powers of enchantment, however, load it with feeling and value and encourage love and attachment to life itself, without which, Bennett asserts, there can be no attachment to anything. Finally, she claims that she "pursues a life with moments of enchantment rather than an enchanted way of life" (p. 10). Hardy's fiction corresponds remarkably to this pursuit, for although it is absurd to claim that the worlds he creates produce "an enchanted way of life," they are filled with "moments of enchantment." Enchantment as a way of life would, in both Darwin's and Hardy's terms, sentimentalize and falsify a nature that goes its way without reference to how we humans feel about it. For any of these writers to minimize the difficulties or the pain would be a betrayal of the life that each loved in the here and now, intensely.

And indeed, the posthumous reputations of Darwin and Hardy do not suggest enchantment at all. "Darwinian," though literally it means only "related to Darwin or Darwin's ideas," usually means "fierce, selfish, competitive, relentless struggle for survival." One doesn't hear much about "Darwinian love" unless love means urge to reproduction and self-perpetuation. One doesn't hear much about "Darwinian selflessness" either (unless it means reciprocal altruism – you scratch my back, I'll scratch yours). "Hardyesque" is nothing like as common a word as "Darwinian," but insofar as it is used it is likely to imply a tragic and chance-driven fatality. As against these popular understandings, however, there is the Darwin that the distinguished historian of science Robert Richards describes: a Darwin who was before all other things a "romantic," a thinker whose ideas emerged from a sense of a value-laden world, progressive and perfectible, and fraught with meaning (the Wordsworthian and Miltonic echoes are everywhere). Neither "progress" nor "perfectibility" plays any role at all in "Darwin's dangerous idea," as it is interpreted by writers as diverse as Daniel Dennett and Stephen Jay Gould. But Richards calls our attention to a different Darwin, one whose prose "vibrated with the poetic appreciation of nature's inner core." He wanted, says Richards, "to deliver to the reader an aesthetic assessment that lay beyond the scientifically articulable."[11]

Hardy's prose too, when it is not simply "on duty," vibrates with poetic appreciation of nature's inner core. It is exceptionally detailed in its perceptions of the varieties of life, but, as we have already seen, it creates an experience very different from what would seem to be entailed by the dark messages that reason and theory require. Hardy affirms life in the act of writing stories that would notoriously deny it.

Romantic visionaries both, neither Hardy nor Darwin began heterodox. Hardy was, the evidence suggests, almost evangelically pious down through the 1850s and 1860s. Darwin was certainly never really pious – given his upbringing as the grandchild of Erasmus Darwin, the once famous scientist and poet of a Lamarckian kind of evolution, and with his very large rationalist father. But he was conventionally religious (and the crew of the *Beagle* teased him for that). If only for practical reasons, he did not, when he left for Cambridge, exclude the possibility of becoming a clergyman. Though both Hardy and Darwin fell famously away from traditional religion, neither became hostile to the Church. Victorian literature is distinctive for its narratives of spiritual crises and conversion, but neither Hardy nor Darwin seems to have gone through such a crisis. Gradually their faith eroded. As we have seen, all his life Hardy was obsessively concerned with "respectability," and remained socially very restrained and conservative, disclaiming (sometimes perhaps disingenuously) any disruptive intention in his writings. It is clear that he felt deeply the loss of the traditional God and loved the church even if he did not believe its dogma. Darwin, sensitive to his wife's piety and socially and morally conservative, always supported though he would not attend the church at Down. He carefully avoided the kind of anticlerical battles that marked the career of T. H. Huxley, Darwin's most aggressive and forceful defender, known for this reason as his "bulldog." And, of course, Darwin was buried in Westminster Abbey.

For both Hardy and Darwin, the most telling criticism of Christian theism was the existence of suffering. Neither could believe that an all-loving and all-knowing God could have been responsible for the horrors

and tragedies of human (and animal) experience. Natural selection mindlessly builds life out of death, and along the way is regardless of the pain
that is built into the process. But it is one thing to explain death and
suffering as part of the necessary process of natural selection (or, as William
Paley had justified it, as essential to human "probation"); it is another to
feel the suffering not as general but as individual, as novelists inevitably
must do. Death is not vaguely statistical; it is personal and individual.
Hardy's sensitivity to the pervasiveness of pain, waste, loss, and suffering
led him to little Father Time's suicide in *Jude the Obscure*. And a vision
such as that is often read into the tired eyes of the long-bearded Darwin, as
they are revealed in late photographs.

And yet the works of both writers reflect the other side of the alertness to
the individual fate: a wonder-inducing attentiveness to the particularities
of life, from "ephemera" and barnacles and worms and ants and slugs to
rabbits and birds and grass and trees – and people. That sharp eye for
particularities that makes Darwin's work so convincing and Hardy's work
so gorgeously painful is closely connected to a strong ethical relation to the
social and natural worlds (and a recognition that "social" and "natural" are
not radically distinct), each driven in his own way into sympathetic
engagement with the creatures they describe – a "feeling for the organ-
ism" – as if they loved them.

Given these odd parallels, it is best to take a good look at the worst
before proceeding – a perfectly Hardyan thing to do. And here is Hardy
looking hard:

> A woeful fact – that the human race is too extremely developed for its
> corporeal conditions, the nerves being evolved to an activity abnormal in
> such an environment. Even the higher animals are in excess in this respect.
> It may be questioned if Nature, or what we call Nature, so far back as when
> she crossed the line from invertebrates to vertebrates, did not exceed her
> mission. This planet does not supply the material for happiness to higher
> existences. (*LWTH*, p. 227)

The obvious bleakness here depends on the anomalous hyperactivity of
human nerves, a hyperactivity that is registered in the plots and narrative
voice of most of Hardy's novels. The preoccupation with seeing, which
I have noted at length in the last chapter, might be seen as the most
extended example of "the nerves being evolved" to "abnormal" activity.
But what makes so many of Hardy's novels movingly beautiful is just this
"recharging" of the nerves, as Bennett puts it. The uncanny perceptiveness
of Hardy's rendering of the natural world is never simply utilitarian – as

Darwin's must often be seen. After all, understanding the way nature works is likely to lead to adaptive behavior. But Hardy's narrators repeatedly teach us to see beyond the limited perspectives of any of the individual consciousnesses that populate his narratives, reminding us of invisible connections, implying mutual dependencies and possible dooms, and suggesting patterns of life, change, and movement that it is art's function to discover and create. As he writes early in *The Woodlanders*, despite the apparent separateness of the lives of his protagonists and the isolation of the little community that is the novel's focus, "their lonely courses formed no detached design at all, but were part of the pattern in the great web of human doings then weaving in both hemispheres, from the White Sea to Cape Horn" (*W*, ch. 3, p. 52). The elements that constitute Hardy's "pessimism" are oddly akin to elements of Darwin's theory. The human race's extreme development implies ultimately a grand vision of connectedness and a subtle sensibility to all forms of life. The famous last paragraph of the *Origin*, climaxing in Darwin's claim for "grandeur in this view of life," treats "the production of the higher animals" as the apex of development from all the apparent mess and awfulness of the process of natural selection – "war of nature . . . famine and death". It concludes in "the most exalted object we are capable of conceiving, namely, the production of the higher animals" (p. 490). For Hardy, while he usually resists deliberately upbeat language, there is a kind of double wonder – first, of course, that the "higher animals" have emerged from this apparent mess, and second, that the human mind has been able to see through the tangle and make sense of it. Such perceptions, provoked by the largely nonadaptive hyperactivity of the nerves, make for a sense of the wonder of life in the heart of Hardy's pessimism.

In *Jude* Hardy on duty tells us, embittered, that "nobody did come, because nobody does," but from his keen attention to the widest possible range of life – the great patterns weaving among the hemispheres, the rabbit screaming, the slugs caught in Tess's gown, the sleeping doves falling into the fire – the wise distant Hardyesque narrator dramatizes in precision and attentiveness strong compassion for all forms of life. Darwin, to take a familiar example, reminds his readers that "the face of nature bright with gladness," in which "the birds . . . are idly singing round us," doesn't immediately reveal to us that the happy birds are devouring other forms of life. Concern shifts to the insects being destroyed. And the singing birds themselves are likely at some point to be destroyed by beasts of prey. Everything will be changing as we move through "all seasons of each recurring year" (p. 62).

It is a passage that, if not quite as poetically focused, might have been written by Hardy himself. It forces us to see more than is immediately visible. It worries the calm of the moment with portents of change, and sets the particular scene in the context of altering time and a broadening range of life. " 'I find no grain,' cries the rook in winter." Yet the darkling thrush, out of season too, breaks out in "full-hearted even-song/Of joy illimited."[12] Although we may hear in Darwin's paragraph connection to the impending glooming ironies of Hardy's narratives, the nature of the language almost always comes as a surprise to first-time readers of the *Origin*. It is strangely novelistic or poetic. The passage leaps off its scientific page because it is built on a feeling for the textures of life, for the pleasures of birdsong, for the release of the springtime – not exactly scientific feelings. Its drama depends on a prior attachment to life. It is not a long way from here to Jude's innocent concern for the crows, the narrator's alertness to the destruction of the snails on which Tess trod, or the sudden revelation of other life – the "ephemera" – when the match for a moment illuminates the evening in *A Pair of Blue Eyes*. Some of the peculiar beauty of Hardy's fictions depends on this Darwinian attentiveness.

That abnormal human nervous activity, manifest in the novels in their Darwinian alertness to nature's ways, is built thematically and stylistically into the texture of Hardy's prose. And while in the passage just quoted Hardy talks about this activity as in excess and thus dangerous, it emerges not only as curse but as something of a blessing. The curse is in the excess of sensitivity that makes his characters (and himself) vulnerable; the blessing (if that it might be called) is in the way it makes possible an understanding of the mindless processes among which we live, and an appreciation of its extraordinary potential for beauty. Hardy's tendency to hide and protect himself also at times acts as celebration. As Lawrence notes – and complains – the novels are full of characters who risk reaching for the intense satisfactions of life. They answer the calls of instinct and desire and aspiration to fullness, but the narratives finally punish them for their daring. In different ways, this is the case for Jude, for Henchard, and even for Giles Winterborne. Clym Yeobright had tasted the possibility of fullness in his imagination of utopian change, and returns to bring it to Egdon Heath. Tess and Angel surrender to the deep sensuousness of their mating season. In all of these novels, aspiration to fullness is frustrated (just as Darwin's birds will be preyed upon by winter and hawks). But the power of natural sensuousness has never been more beautifully evoked than in the sequences in *Tess* in which the two lovers are irresistibly attracted to each other. The novels evoke the experience of fullness even as the stories themselves put such experience just beyond the protagonists' grasp.

Hardy's fiction might be seen as both expression of and homage to what the "nerves" reveal, almost, as it were, to the "nerves" themselves, for they are nature's excess, what gives humans their eccentric, self-conscious power to see and feel beyond the mere adaptive utility that seems essential for survival under the reign of natural selection. They are homage to and expression of the human capacity to feel, react, and imagine. Through the voices of the narrators and behind them through Hardy himself, his novels give shape to the apparently random and chancy movements of life, and create an art that will trace the figure in the carpet and embody a series of what Hardy called "seemings." By creating narrators who see intensely but remain, in their language and style, outside the dramas that ensnare and inflict pain on those who yield to the call of their desire and passion, Hardy might be thought almost to approximate in fiction that "objectivity" that Darwin sought in his science.

Staid, defensive, conservative Victorian gentlemen, Hardy and Darwin, reputedly radical and iconoclast in their work, believed that the world was something like a tangled bank, regardless of human needs and principles of order, constructed from mindless processes.[13] The order that humans have perceived before this insight and continue to perceive is an order totally constructed by the hypersensitive and nonadaptive human mind – through science and through art. What makes humans distinctively human are just the nonadaptive things that increase the likelihood of pain and loss, the hypersensitivity that allows the shaping work of the mind, the turning into art and meaning a world that, in effect, means nothing but itself. For Darwin, the form of his discourse entailed a full commitment to exclusive rationality, although his prose is charged with feeling. His work is part of the continuing effort of modern science to naturalize everything, including the human spirit itself. It is part of the great "rationalization and intellectualization" of life. But part of that work, as clear in Darwin as it is in Freud, was that of recognizing and trying to understand the irrational – rationally. This entailed alertness to the affective (and therefore moral) implications of his arguments.

A careful reading of Darwin reveals not only the outlines of the world-historical theory but also moral engagement with its significance. The efforts at full rational explanation are often couched in language that responds to the emotional and moral commitments that drove his work and his life. In the consolatory passage in "The Struggle for Existence," Darwin was directly addressing the emotional rather than the intellectual responses to his theory. Written by Hardy, it would be bitterly ironic, but in both cases the concern is with moral implications, not fact. Though committed to an objective and disinterested rendering of their subjects, refusing to allow moral priorities to shape what they saw or how they would describe it, both Hardy and Darwin felt the urgency of the ethical problems their visions provoked. Darwin tried again in *The Descent of Man* to introduce consolatory moral considerations into his arguments, and with more success. There he argues that morality itself is built into the natural system – humans as social animals will inevitably have to develop an ethical imperative. But this could do little to eliminate the sense that the whole process of natural selection is merciless and mindless, and it appears that Hardy's reading of it was as bleak as Darwin feared: the novels might be read in one respect as controlled rages on behalf of the suffering *individuals* caught up in this universal struggle, the struggle in which, Darwin had claimed, death is mercifully quick.

Darwin never raged against the universe, but for him as well as for Hardy, moral framing of that amoral world was necessary. In *The Descent of Man*, although he insists that the differences between apes and humans is not in kind but in degree, Darwin begins his discussion of the moral sense by agreeing that "of all the differences between man and the lower animals, the moral sense or conscience is by far the most important."[4] He takes his task to be to discuss that distinctive human quality from the perspective of natural history. Although he never publicly discusses the issue in this way, what he discovers in nature is incompatible with the imagination of a loving God, and most particularly, once again, because in the midst of all the wonders of nature there is pain and death everywhere.

Both Darwin and Hardy put their arguments for unbelief in compassionate and moral terms. They were both peculiarly sensitive to the pain of others. The Christian God can't exist as he is described because no loving god could be so immoral as to produce the system whose horrors Darwin tries to minimize. One can doubt that his own consoling paragraph in his chapter on "The Struggle for Existence" provided him much consolation. There was no easing the pain or justifying the death of his beloved and innocent daughter, Annie, at ten years old. Nor was her death very quick. In his memoir of her, Darwin looked back by emphasizing her capacity for joy and life – "the main feature in her disposition which at once rises before me is her buoyant joyousness tempered by . . . her sensitiveness . . . and her strong affection." Darwin proceeds to record with quite tender particularity the various ways Annie behaved, helped, loved, cuddled. Concluding the memoir, he returns to the theme: "But looking back, always the spirit of joyousness rises before me as her emblem and characteristic: she seemed formed to live a life of happiness."[15] With the eyes that saw Annie die, he was describing a world in which life depended on death.

The happy ending, except in a few of the earlier novels (and "happy" may not quite be the word, even for *The Hand of Ethelberta* or *A Laodicean* or *Far from the Madding Crowd*), is not part of Hardy's vision. One of the crises of Victorian secularizing was the difficulty of finding a way to represent the world truthfully while continuing to represent it as laden with value. For most students of Victorian literature, the point of reference for this kind of problem is George Eliot. Although by the time she was writing novels, George Eliot had long since lost faith in the literal truth of Christianity, she clung to its moral truth, to the truth of feeling. She works at resolution to the problem in her second novel, *The Mill on the Floss*, in a deliberately tragic way, with the drowning of her heroine, Maggie. There could be no providential reversal within the secular terms in which George Eliot was imagining the world of her characters, but Maggie is morally triumphant, and as George Eliot puts it in the last pages, "Nature repairs her ravages."[16] There is the possible inference that somehow, built into nature, there was not only a natural cycle of rebirth but also a moral order. Natural processes and human, moral ones, were compatible.

It was but a short step from there to Hardy's final rejection of the possibility that moral order is built into the natural world. Completely naturalized, his world notoriously moves regardless of any human conception of justice and morality. It is Darwin's world without Darwin's efforts to reconcile it to traditional Christian moral order. In George Eliot one can almost always detect a principle of Nemesis built into natural law: somehow in the very nature of things rough justice is at work, and evil will eventually be punished. Nemesis catches up with Arthur Donnithorne in *Adam Bede* and punishes him for his liaison with Hetty Sorrel. But if in George Eliot the bad guys continue to be punished in a world of secular order, in Hardy the good guys are punished as well, particularly as Lawrence insists, when they dare to act reckless of the rules of respectability. George Eliot finds the traditional happy endings very hard to replicate, but she builds a secular theory of consequences that is both empiricist and ethical: our deeds determine us as much as we determine our deeds.

For Hardy, to put it simply, that game was up: his narratives imply that there is no relation in moral value between deeds and their consequences (unless it is a reverse one). If there is something like spiritual value and balance in the world, it is behind those nerves, that is, in human consciousness. This does not mean that his books are any less morally urgent and self-conscious than George Eliot's. Behind them lies not only a longing for a traditional understanding and justice but also an enhanced sense of the possibilities of fullness, the life full of life that Darwin saw in his lost daughter. Order and meaning, he will realize, is the product of human consciousness, of human art.

As we have seen, however, rather than reading the consequences of Darwinian thinking as amoral (and disenchanting), Hardy derived from Darwin an even more intensely moral understanding of relationships. The difficulties of the natural processes and the connectedness that they demonstrate entail a greater concern for all living things than even Christian morality required. Darwin's love of animals is as obvious and overt as Hardy's. It is true that he fought for the right of vivisection and gave priority to human life over animal life; that commitment was moral as well as scientific. Much of his theory is driven by a moral sympathy that becomes evident in the uses to which he put his imaginative understanding of the sensibility of everything – barnacles and ants and worms and wasps and spiders and pheasants and apes. His love of dogs is well documented. His awe at the powers of the smallest living things to make enormous changes in our visible world was a crucial part of the equipment by which he turned gradualism into a convincing explanation of the way the world works. Hardy's inference from Darwin's vision is perfectly consistent with Darwin's own. The Golden Rule lies at the moral end of Darwin's scientific journey.

Hardy was obviously *not* a moralist in his fiction. Ruth Yeazell reminds us of his resistance to moralism, quoting Reuben Dewy of *Under the Greenwood Tree* as saying, "If the story-tellers could ha' got decency and good morals from true stories, who'd have troubled to invent parables?" Yeazell goes on, "Dewy's contention that 'all true stories have a coarse touch or a bad moral' provides a working definition of realism that . . . seems very close to Hardy's own."[17] It is not that reality's narratives yield the moral Hardy draws from Darwin, but that the exigencies of material life require from the human mind and spirit yet greater moral energy. Your neighbor is biologically your brother, and you owe to the trapped rabbit or the impaled horse a deep moral debt. Although through Dewy Hardy may be arguing that truthful art must always have something coarse about it (we know Hardy's relation to the unofficial but shamefully compromising censorship of polite literature), he obviously does not regard this as diminishing the moral function of art. Art, it might be said, is a charging of the nerves, a heightening of and a prod to human's extra-adaptive

hyperactive brain, and as such it brings beauty and morality into syn-
chrony. Art brings order to a world that is regardless of it; it makes
beautiful what, in the processes of natural selection, has the merely
utilitarian function of breeding and survival. It is part of the morality of
art to register the ordinary with the most vivid particularity, to discover it
though it might be hidden in the most unlikely of places, to honor it, to
recognize the wonder in the ordinariness, and finally to make us feel our
connection to it.

Many of these qualities of Hardy's work and life, reflecting also the
sensibility and attitudes of Darwin, are present in the wonderful sheep-
shearing scene in *Far from the Madding Crowd*. Here one can feel that
capacity for joy of which Gillian Beer talks, and which is implicit in
Darwin's sad celebration of his daughter's life. The sheep-shearing
takes place in a building as old as the medieval churches in the area,
perhaps once part of the "conventual buildings" of the era.
The architect Hardy speaks warmly of the structures of these simple
buildings, which show "the origin of grandeur not apparent in erec-
tions where mere ornamentation has been attempted." The place is
steeped in its own history, which is reflected in its perfect adaptation to
the work being done there: "the purpose which had dictated its original
erection was the same with that to which it was still applied." It is
a human construction, but "natural" as well – the spirit of the ancient
builders was at one with the spirit of the modern beholder: it is, in
effect, a holy place, and if one wonders how Hardy's persistent feeling
for religion expressed itself, it was in such places and passages as this,
where the secularity is deeply religious:

> Standing before this abraded pile the eye regarded its present usage, the
> mind dwelt upon its past history, with a satisfied sense of functional
> continuity throughout, a feeling almost of gratitude, and quite of pride, at
> the permanence of the idea which heaped it up. The fact that four centuries
> had neither proved it to be founded on a mistake, inspired any hatred of its
> purpose, nor given rise to any reaction that had battered it down, invested
> this simple grey effort of old minds with a repose if not a grandeur which
> a too curious reflection was apt to disturb in its ecclesiastical and military
> compeers ... The defence and salvation of the body by daily bread is still
> a study, a religion, and a desire. (ch. 22, p. 127)

These are perfectly Darwinian sentiments – the recognition of a history in
a heap of organized stones, the teasing out of a past, the movement through
a series of transformative uses as one form of life affirms itself by transforming into another, equally useful. The fundamental material conditions

survive the contingencies of history, and the deep past is recognizable in the present, however transformed it might be.

Hardy's way of seeing and feeling suggests an evolutionary story. It is the "church" that is "battered down," while this brilliantly simple structure, adapted to humans' natural needs, survives. The pleasures of life, particularly the visual, glitter through this only apparently peculiar instance of adaptation – "the barn was natural to the shearers, and the shearers were in harmony with the barn." The strong and useful architecture makes of the "braded pile" a new, a secular church, surviving because it answers to human needs, as transformed species answer to the needs Darwin had laid out in his theory. The art, the architecture, harbors and sustains life.

"What are my books," Hardy asked, "but one plea against 'man's inhumanity to man' – to woman – and to the lower animals."[18] Although this is one of Hardy's deliberate, defensive, and perhaps over-simplifying explanations of his art, there is a very real sense in which it is also true. Hardy's sensitivity to the lives of animals is explicit and pervasively perceptible in his novels, and art is the place where the "nerves" we shouldn't need for simple natural selection alert us and evoke compassion for the lives of others. Those nerves that expose us all to so much pain are essential because the Darwinian world Hardy experienced had nothing to do with the fundamentally anthropocentric explanatory modes of traditional religion and even of science. Those "seemings," which describe in such bleak and strictly formal organization the way nature and society worked, gave aesthetic shape to the tangled bank, and made a new kind of meaning, which emerges from Hardy's singular attention to the ordinary.

Despite the implicitly angry subtitle of *Tess*, "A Pure Woman Faithfully Presented," his books, sometimes written with great moral energy, tend not to be moralized. The subtitle of *Tess*: "A Pure Woman Faithfully Presented by Thomas Hardy," while consistent with Hardy's vision throughout his novels, is an aberration in its implicitly bitter moral irony. His persistent dramatization of the social and moral disasters caused by the class system, which culminate in *Jude*, obviously carry a strong animus. But the novels are never argumentative or ideologically driven; Hardy was not being disingenuous when, in usual authorial ways, he disclaimed such merely ideological intention and insisted on the aesthetic integrity of his fictions. Whatever the ideological or moral work they might be thought to be doing, they are "enchanting," gorgeous patterns in the carpet, but more. There runs through them all a particular relish for things of this world, reverence for the varieties and abundance of life, reverence for life itself. This is even true in the last heavily ironic moments of *Tess*, that memorable scene in which Tess falls asleep as a kind of sacrifice on a Stonehenge slab:

> The band of silver paleness along the east horizon made even the distant parts of the Great plain appear dark and near, the whole enormous land-scape bore that impress of reserve, taciturnity, and hesitation which is usual before day. The eastward pillars and their architraves stood up blackly against the light, and the great flame-shaped Sun-stone beyond them, and the stone of sacrifice midway. Presently, the night died out, and the quiver-ing little pools in the cup-like hollows of the stones lay still. (ch. 58, p. 381)

Here the Hardyan understory emerges to reshape the significance of the tragedy. At first what is most striking is the vastness of the landscape culminating in the sharp chiaroscuro and silence in the last moments of pre-dawn and "the great flame-shaped Sun-stone beyond." But what makes this passage most distinctly Hardyan is the subtlety of perception, mixing the geometrical precision of architectural language with the deli-cacy of the registration of "cup-like hollows" in the stones, and the ways in which water gathers in remnants of the past, quivering in slight breezes and stilled by the new day: this is the language of a poet in love with the way the world feels and looks, and sensitive to its contrasts, its pasts.

It is with such juxtapositions and details that he sets the stage for the disrupting appearance of the police, who come to take Tess away. The passage is thick with the past, with centuries of erosion and further centuries in which the structure served, ironically, for similar sacrifices. If setting Tess up on an ancient sacrificial stone is another of the excesses of Hardy's narrative ironies, that excess is redeemed by the delicate registra-tion of large movements of time, of small details of the moment, and the juxtaposition of the vitality of Tess's now warmly quiet body with the stone and history. If one rebels against Hardy's heavy plotting, one surrenders (at least I surrender) to those "quivering little pools in the cup-like hollows of the stones" and the felt stillness of the air when night gives way to morning. The scene itself, whatever the elaborations of the plotting, appropriately honors Tess's purity, which has always been sensuous.

It also, perhaps most obviously, registers the sanctity of the body and of the secular in a place originally created for religious purposes. It is an enchanted moment in which the certainly implicit anger at the waste of a lovely wronged woman is only tacit, and it follows a rare sequence in Hardy when, however briefly, the doomed lovers achieve the fullness of consummation that escapes almost all other of his protagonists. The "President of the Immortals" spoils the delicacy of the writing, which implicitly evokes something quite different from this ironically conceived tyrant – the gorgeous movements of time, the vitality and warmth of nature's narrative for that moment, at dawn. But Hardy's turn to that commentary does not cancel the love for the sleeping woman and for the deep past and the glories of dawn.

It is one of the typical Hardy moments in which the novel does the work that Bennett discusses when she insists on the possibility of secular enchantment. The religious strain in Hardy did not die away. It just took a different shape. He continued to seek "fullness," and human flourishing, and he wrote, "let us magnify good works and develop all means of easing mortals' progress through a world not worthy of them" (*Life and Work*, p. 358). Hardy's "good works" are his art, his novels, his poems. It may be ironic that one of the ways that Hardy found to "ease mortals' progress through the world" was to write stories that described how very difficult that progress is. But it is in the language Hardy found – what Amy King, in another context, calls "reverent form," that is, in reverent attention to the most minute details of the vital material world, in sympathetic notation of its inevitable pain, and in the organization of the complexity of that tangled bank in which we are all caught up with one another, that Hardy at his Darwinian best emerges.

The moral sense growing from Hardy's recognition of the implications of Darwin's theory – we are all literally brothers and sisters under the skin – gives Hardy's full look at the worst its force. Like Darwin, Hardy could not look at the mindless processes of the world without feeling the pain that they must inflict on conscious beings. Against the interpretation that Darwin's rationalization and intellectualization of the world had stripped it of meaning and value, he saw that it was just those consciousnesses that created meaning. Hardy looks with Darwinian eyes and re-enchants the world.

CHAPTER 3

The Mayor of Casterbridge
Reversing the Real

In *The Mayor of Casterbridge* the dark villain is already almost the hero.

D. H. Lawrence

The Mayor of Casterbridge might be taken as Hardy's most elaborate and complex expression of the doubleness that haunts all of his works: the shame that drives his protagonists toward conventionality and respectability, and the vital energy of desire that irrationally drives them into a life of perilous irregularity. Inevitably, the consequence is disaster, but *The Mayor of Casterbridge* gives to Michael Henchard, its protagonist, a tragic stature that affirms the very dangerous energies to which he succumbs.

Lawrence complains that Hardy "makes every exceptional person a villain, all exceptional or strong individual traits he holds up as weaknesses or wicked faults" (*P*, p. 436). Henchard is one of Lawrence's favored exceptions, perhaps the fullest developed example of Hardy protagonists who embody something of the vital energy that is so often confined to the understory. He marks Hardy's most decisive and interesting turn from the Laodicean way, "lukewarm, and neither hot nor cold,"[1] of resolving his fictions. The Laodicean way, which he obviously dramatized in his own, *A Laodicean*, might well be taken as an example, acted out thematically and unfortunately, in the overall quality of the narrative. Hardy always partly resists the mode of Victorian realism in which he works, insisting that his stories are only "seemings," while at the same time he punishes, as Victorian realism punishes, the protagonists who break out from the ordinary. It is true that the last half of *The Mayor of Casterbridge* excruciatingly and symmetrically punishes Henchard for his outbreak, tracing his tormented ambition, his startling rise and inexorable fall, his conflicted but powerful desires, through to his decline into the nothingness of the final pages. He sells his wife; he lies; he develops a passionate male friendship and seeks revenge passionately: almost villainous, almost heroic. He emerges in all his capacity for instability and excess an "exceptional," if radically flawed, figure, worthy of the self-consciously tragic form Hardy finds for his story. The novel at once celebrates and retreats in fear from his recklessness of convention, and so does Henchard himself, whose notorious reversals of his own decisions and commitments mark every movement of the plot. Henchard plays out dramatically what the novel manifests everywhere – tension between the conventional and the life-giving, between respectability and daring, between mere acquiescence in social order and deep feeling for life itself.

Although Henchard's desires dominate the narrative and give it its form, the novel in effect is a drama about the price of daring to live, as Hardy feared it. The Lawrentian Hardy will always be defeated as the narratives wind to their bleak ends, but Henchard's story sustains ambivalence and concludes in a kind of dark heroism. Here is a strong, if powerfully ironic, example of the affirmation of Lawrentian life implicit in Hardy's representation of character and natural ambience. For Henchard the hero wills his own death. Although Hardy did not want to be caught out as Reuben Dewy's voice of "bad morals," the figure of Henchard implies such a voice even as it opts to extinguish itself. While Hardy's sense of life almost always requires such a voice, he also almost invariably compromises into the tradition of Victorian realism. But *The Mayor of Casterbridge* is one of his novels on the brink of disrupting dominant aesthetic and moral conventions, on the brink of becoming fully what appealed to Lawrence about him: the representation of a world in which human behavior is largely determined by irrational forces within and without, forces that need to be honored, not repressed, and that are frequently represented in Hardy's descriptions of the animal life that lies just outside of the drama. While Tennyson could pray, "Let the ape and the tiger die," Hardy could never kill them, and seems not to have wanted to. His novels evoke strong feeling for characters whom he would never emulate, who allow desire and ambition to lead them to violate the social rules. His protagonists, from Dick Dewy to Michael Henchard, are all, in some respects, quite ordinary; yet they increasingly become focuses of tragic intensity. Their desires are not romantic dreams to be mocked and minimized by wise or ironic narrators, but the stuff of nature and of tragedy.

In Hardy Victorian realism turns away from the comic form of compromise, which normally brings hero and heroine together after the fantasies and dreams of youth are expelled. That realism, which in England resolves in a (sometimes qualified) happy ending, is marked primarily by an implicit rejection of extremes for the complicated and compromised norms of Victorian middle-class culture. There are any number of moments of disenchantment that mark mainstream Victorian realist fiction: the disenchanted acceptance of the ordinary and emergence into the sharp sunlight that banishes the fantasies of romance; the recognition of the needs of others and of the limitations of the self; the revelation like Gwendolen Harleth's, in George Eliot's *Daniel Deronda*, that "her horizon was but a dipping onward of an existence with which her own was revolving";[2] the discovery of one's own mixed nature, of the flaws in one's lover, of the insuperable pressures of society. In Hardy these moments of disenchantment become not less inevitable, but less a means to moral growth, and less adequate as a summary of reality.

Hardy's novels become almost unendurable occasions for social tragedy, as he cannot allow those who dare to engage the broader morality of nature itself to survive. The novels give the impression that, although the narrator does what he can to minimize them, the stakes have been raised, not only far beyond the norm of Victorian realism, but also to the level of the absolute. His world is charged with meanings and significances that only the keen-eyed characters and the narrator can grasp, and it is exigent. There are, to be sure, characters in his novels who make the compromise, but most of Hardy's protagonists seem to echo the experience of Victor Frankenstein, whose history is a sequence of waverings between an absolute idea and a domestic compromise. One feels, retrospectively, a Hardyan quality to Frankenstein's last uncompromising recovery of his dream amid the vision of failures: "Yet another may succeed."[3]

In *The Woodlanders*, Dr. Edred Fitzpiers retreats to a country practice, with vague ideas of doing important research, just as in *Middlemarch*, published 15 years earlier, Dr. Tertius Lydgate had retreated to a small town so as to be free for what he imagined might be major medical research. The stories parallel each other, but their effects are completely different. When Fitzpiers contemplates marrying Grace Melbury and settling in Little Hintock, he asks himself,

> Why should he go further into the world than where he was? The secret of happiness lay in limiting the aspirations: these men's thoughts were coterminous with the margin of the Hintock woodlands, and why should not his be likewise limited – a small practice among the people around him being the bound of his desires. (*W*, ch. 19, p. 167)

What might in an earlier novel have been the disenchanted revelation of the inevitability and virtue of limits is for Fitzpiers an untenable dream. Unlike Lydgate's story, which almost rises to the tragic even inside the ordinariness of the town, Fitzpiers's story virtually parodies such serious-ness. Fitzpiers has no potential for serious work; what is at play in his story is the irrational pull of sexuality and desire and, of course, snobbishness. The transformation of the small and the ordinary into materials for tragic drama doesn't happen, and it is as though Fitzpiers's story makes fun of Victorian realism's seriousness. What matters is the degree to which it is safe to indulge desire. Elizabeth-Jane, at the end of *The Mayor of Casterbridge*, reflects similarly and with the authority of the narrative itself on the dark limits of life, but in Fitzpiers, these thoughts of resignation are ironic, almost comic, given his anomalous, quasi-aristocratic, and relatively amoral character. It's as though he is engaged in intellectual slumming.

Immediately after he does in fact marry Grace, he falls in love with the richer and more "modern" Mrs. Charmond. The woodspeople, whose thoughts were "coterminous" with the woods, are themselves a dying breed. Although an anomaly at Hintock, the volatile and unstable Fitzpiers, who couldn't possibly internalize the limits he seems ready to choose, is too shallow to be regarded as Promethean. The compromises he is forced to make at the end of the novel in returning to Grace diminish him; when Grace accepts him again, the novel leaves only Marty South with the dignity of the woodland traditions, able to remain true to her impossible ideal. (Yet there is irony here, too, for Marty's loyalty is another aspect of her childlessness. There is no future for those who remain unchanging, even unchangingly loyal, while the "flexibility" of both Fitzpiers and Grace – however shallow morally they may be – guarantees them at least some kind of future. Adaptability is survival. They are both, after all, Laodiceans.) The novel implies no growth that comes with compromise, or that is its mark. Compromise here, in contrast to the Victorian realist tradition, means only loss of the little dignity Fitzpiers had in the authenticity of his passion.

Thus if Hardy, by way of Elizabeth-Jane, would seem to endorse the notion that the "secret of happiness lay in limiting the aspiration,"[4] *The Mayor of Casterbridge* implies that the secret of both good fiction and life is refusal to compromise and pushing the limits of aspiration as far as they can be pushed. Happiness is not a normal or safe human condition. The characters who aspire absurdly and beyond the control of their own will have a quality of heroism that distinguishes them impressively from those Laodiceans who have not answered the deep call of desire or aspired beyond the security of their station. We have seen that Hardy's narrative voice keeps him aloofly distinguished from the passions it describes, and so it does in *The Mayor of Casterbridge*, remaining almost archaeologically disengaged from the action, protected from it so thoroughly that Hardy can afford to release within the narrative precisely those energies that earlier realists, in their compassionate focus on the details and surfaces of ordinary experience, kept submerged. The self-denial of Thomas Carlyle's "Everlasting Yea," which might be taken as the ideology of the Victorian realist novelist's world (it is what the repentant Sue Bridehead harks back to), is not in Hardy a tough-minded acceptance of a limiting reality. Rather, it is an act of self-protection, felt in the narrator's own refusal to engage himself, and yet largely and tragically inaccessible to the actors in his dramas. It is unnatural in life, requiring extraordinary discipline of will and feeling, and it is probably unsustainable. Self-denial is itself a romantic dream, and its consequences can be destructive.

The primary reality among many of Hardy's protagonists is the desire that drives them, usually for a beautiful woman or a dashing man like Sergeant Troy in *Far from the Madding Crowd*, but sometimes also beyond – Swithin's ambition in *Two on a Tower* to be an astronomer, Clym's in *Return of the Native* to be a teacher, Jude's to be a scholar. The large aspirations that mark the romantic hero, which are manifested in Victor Frankenstein with catastrophic and in Tertius Lydgate with pathetic results, are not, for Hardy, rare exceptions to the human norm. They can manifest themselves anywhere; they can be felt, in small, in Dick Dewy's love of Fancy Day and Giles Winterborne's love of Grace. Whereas realism gets much of its original thrust from a comic and ironic view of romantic aspiration, Hardy treats aspiration neither as an aberration nor a falsification, but as representatively, critically, tragically human. The qualities that distinguish the human from the merely natural are the hypersensitivity and intelligence that are, in the Darwinian terms that Hardy understood, beyond what is necessary for adaptation. The human in Hardy is the only element in nature that makes itself incompatible with it.

Hardy saw a world that was at once continuous with yet in almost every major respect the reverse of the world projected with moral rigor, sincerity, and tough-mindedness by the Victorian realists. The Hardyesque landscape stands in sharp contrast to the rural scenes of a majority of Victorian novels. It is not always pretty; it does not always surge with meanings ultimately relevant to the condition of the characters but usually with meanings that transcend them and the plots themselves. The violence of the natural world will intrude into the flattest landscapes; and the upland stretches of Egdon Heath, "a vast tract of unenclosed wild," the hill above Weydon-Priors where Henchard sells his wife, the height from which Jude spies the distant lights of Christminster, the cliff from which Knight perilously hangs – all these release uncontrollable psychic energies. Hardy creates a world that might stand as parodic antithesis to such landscapes as those of Trollope's Barchester or George Eliot's Loamshire, even while they might at any point be taken as literally identical. In *The Mayor of Casterbridge* one can feel something of these vital landscapes at work in the character of Henchard.

That landscape is antithetical, for one thing, in respect to the rules of civilized living and to the notion that civilization is both more interesting and more important than the more primitive world it has displaced. Hardy traces that earlier world in the living rural communities he writes about, in the ruins and ancient structures he habitually describes, and in the abundant and vital natural world. Civilization, his narratives demonstrate, is an arbitrarily acquired and extremely thin veneer over those natural energies that are the quintessentially human. The human, moreover, is both natural and hostile to nature, and is both material and ideal. The rules of society do not adequately cover the variety and complexity of experience. In Hardy they become painfully constraining forces, shaping lives and destroying them. The conventions in Hardy exist not as a general ideal on which variations must be played, but as a human fiction that is both necessary for society and destructive of its most interesting members. The world does not correspond to human need, bringing individual and social together. But human need is itself divided and self-destructive, requiring both the protection of society and freedom from its restraints.

The antithesis implicit in Hardy's attitude to the rules manifests itself as well in his choice of subjects. The long tradition in all Western literature and in realistic fiction of the comic use of peasants and rustics also gives them a choral function. They comment on the central action, warn of its consequences, express social norms, and their lives tend to be imagined as light echoes of the more literate protagonists. In Scott we find a world of rustics who have the vitality and authenticity of unselfconsciously transmitted tradition. They frequently have a fictional life richer than that of the aristocratic heroes and heroines. In George Eliot, rustics often appear to comment shrewdly on the blindnesses of the protagonists and to invoke traditional wisdom with choric force, so as to impose a traditional pattern on the realist's potential disaster.

In Hardy, however, although the tradition of both Scott and George Eliot is at work, the focus is distributed so that rustics and protagonists often blend into each other; rustics might well be protagonists. Clym Yeobright and Grace Melbury are only two who are educated beyond their class and are variously pulled back into it. Hardy tended to see society from the bottom up, as in *The Hand of Ethelberta* where the traditional Richardsonian *Pamela* story emerges again, but with a Pamela who consciously aspires to the status of her Lord B, and is not above deceit:

> All persons who have thoughtfully compared class with class – and the wider their experience the more pronounced their opinion – are convinced that education has as yet but little broken or modified the waves of human impulse on which deeds and words depend. So that in the portraiture of scenes in any way emotional or climactic – the highest province of fiction – the peer and peasant stand on much the same level; the woman who makes the satin train and the woman who wears it. In the lapse of countless ages, no doubt, improved systems of oral education will considerably and appreciably elevate even the involuntary instincts of human nature; but at present culture has only affected the surface of those lives with which it has come in contact, bending down the passions of those predisposed to turmoil as by a silken thread only, which the first ebullition suffices to break. With regard to what may be termed the minor key of action and speech – the unemotional every-day doings of men – social refinement operates upon character in a way which is oftener than not prejudicial to vigorous portraiture, by making the exterior of their screen rather than their index, as with untutored mankind.[5]

Although one detects here a tone of condescension on the part of the autodidact, the passage registers well Hardy's sense that the veneer of civilization has done little to repress the "ebullition" of the irrational that tends to guide everyone's behavior.

A tension develops in Hardy between the irrational powers that threaten social and psychic stability and the aesthetic shape he gives to his narratives. His preoccupation with perspective is one of the formal elements that keep him from being Lawrence. Hardy is preoccupied with the shape of his narratives, which so often threaten to explode but are constrained by an almost mathematical symmetrical form.

Finding in tragedy a model for his narratives is a logical consequence of the new preoccupation with narrative structure. In some well-known notes on fiction Hardy laid out several propositions that help clarify how he had moved to a more "modern" preoccupation with structure.

> The real if unavowed, purpose of fiction is to give pleasure by gratifying the love of the uncommon in human experience, mental or corporeal.
>
> This is done all the more perfectly in proportion as the reader is illuded to believe the personages true and real like himself.
>
> Solely to the latter end a work of fiction should be a precise transcript of ordinary life: but

The uncommon would be absent and the interest lost. Hence,
The writer's problem is, how to strike the balance between the uncommon and the ordinary so to on the one hand to give interest, on the other to
give reality.
In working out this problem, human nature must never be made abnormal, which is introducing incredibility. The uncommonness must be in the
events, not in the characters, and the writer's art lies in shaping that uncommonness while disguising its unlikelihood, if it be unlikely. (*LWTH*, p. 154)

The "uncommon," the "ordinary," "transcript," "illusion" – these are
familiar, but Hardy has somehow rearranged them. His argument for
realism is, in effect, an argument against realism, for Hardy's strategy of
realism "illudes," it disguises unlikelihood. Here is another version of the
dualism between the respectability Hardy always sought and the violation
of decorum through assertions of desire that he admired. The aesthetic
stance further protects Hardy from the dangers of that desire.

His actual practice seems to correspond to this argument, and
The Mayor of Casterbridge, in a mere recital of its events, would seem
absurd; yet from it Henchard emerges with overwhelming conviction.
The love of the "uncommon" that Hardy attributes to his readers is, surely,
his own love, and the "ordinary" world as he imagines it disguises in its
conventionalism (and respectability) a world of intensities and extremes.
"Romanticism," he had written a few months earlier, "will exist in human
nature as long as human nature itself exists."[6]

"A precise transcript of ordinary life," a phrase that echoes so sharply
George Eliot's discussion of the novelist's responsibility in Chapter 17 of
Adam Bede, will never be precisely precise – as George Eliot knew and
claimed. It will always reflect the distortions that result from limitation or
angle of vision or bias. As Hardy was to say much later in his defense of *Jude
the Obscure*, the work of a novelist is "simply an endeavour to give shape
and coherence to a series of seemings, or personal impressions, the question
of their consistency or their discordance, of their permanence or their
transitoriness, being regarded as not of the first moment" (*JO*, p. 39).
Virginia Woolf quotes approvingly a comment Hardy made in the preface
to the fifth edition of *Tess*: "A novel is an impression, not an argument"
(*VW*, p. 230). Hardy will strive to tell the truth, but a Paterian truth, not
the thing as in itself it really is, but the thing as it seems to me to be.

Woolf's admiration of Hardy had something to do with this "impressionism," which is akin to the recurring insight of most of his work,
discussed in the previous chapter, that perspective determines the direction
of the narrative, a protective window glass, an opening to other lives.

Woolf is struck, as Lawrence was, by Hardy's extraordinary attention to the life beyond the protagonists and resistant to the idea that the intentional thrusts of his narratives are adequate to the possibilities of meaning his representation (his impressions) of the ambient world seem to signify. She quotes him again: "Unadjusted impressions have their value, and the road to a true philosophy of life seems to lie in humbly recording diverse readings of its phenomena as they are forced upon us by chance and change."[7]

In the end, then, as I will be arguing more extensively in later chapters, Hardy is closer to writers in the aesthetic movement than is usually noticed. Art is – and ought to be – something other than reality. He seeks organicism and relevance (in his defense of *Jude* he almost gives up "relevance") in his fictions, and in this respect, he is radically, at least in intention, at odds with all the realists who preceded him and with his belated admirer, Lawrence, himself. George Eliot, knowing it was impossible, struggled for the most objective possible stance in relation to reality. Hardy, knowing it was impossible, takes fictional reality to be a series of seemings, of impressions. He develops to an extreme the novelists' sense that experience and history may in the long run be without meaning or value. For Hardy it is precisely the disorder of experience that requires the order of art. Value is human; it does not inhere in nature. While Darwin obviously lies behind Hardy's vision, he seeks a more unstable image: "History is rather a stream than a tree. There is nothing organic in its shape, nothing systematic in its development. It flows on like a thunderstorm-rill by the road-side; now a straw turns it this way, now a tiny barrier of sand that" (*MMB*, p. 247). The artist makes form and meaning.

Against this modern, post-evolutionary vision, Hardy sets his art, which is in constant tension with life in motion. For Hardy, art is the place where structures can be created against the "crass casualty" of history. The novelist hides behind his language and peeks out into the wilderness and savagery that contends in human nature with the constructed ideals of society. Hardy shares the very Darwinian realist sense of how every climax becomes only a moment in a process, and thus of how the dream of permanent closure is misguided in all respects but that of death. "It is the on-going – i.e., the 'becoming' of the world that produces its sadness," says Hardy. "If the world stood still at a felicitous moment there would be no sadness in it" (*LWTH*, p. 210). A novelist like Thackeray, more ironic than most of the Victorians, retreats into the guise of the sage old disenchanted figure whose narrative strategy is to deflate each climactic moment as it comes, but Hardy moves even further from the action in his distinctively labored and distant voice and yet produces dramas of desire and will, focusing on moments of passion with tragic clarity and intensity. As against the lover's attempt to freeze happiness permanently in death, as in Browning's odd poem, "Porphyria's Lover," Hardy describes a world full of protagonists who risk death in dangerous affirmations of vitality through desire. His protection from a similar fate is art itself. His commitment to "realism" remains explicit, but by the time he is done with it, it becomes very much another thing. In one formulation he claims that the novelist's obligation is to "express truly the view of life prevalent in its time," and "the most natural method of presenting them, the method most in accordance with the views themselves, seems to be by a method impassive in its tone and tragic in its developments."[8]

The "impassivity" Hardy advocates suggests something of the defensive maneuvering required of his narrators, whose voices imply the discovery that the limiting of aspirations is not a morally healthy repression of pre-civilized human energy, but directly contrary to the human condition. Such repression cannot end in comic compromise, but only in violent explosions of irrational energy. With all his self-consciousness about the indifference of the universe, Hardy could never imagine an anti-art which, in its own dissolutions of traditional forms, would mimic the dissolution of meaning in the universe. Instead, he aspires both in his novels and his later poetry to maintain a rigorous formal organization, inside of which the relentless and formless passions of desire are contained.

Beyond the disastrous failures of a nature ever completing itself, never complete, of a world incompatible with human intelligence, there remains the power and dignity of the human itself. Such power can *make* the world relevant by imposing on it human intelligence: the story of Michael Henchard, a not distant cousin to Wordsworth's Michael, dramatizes the way human desire virtually creates reality by exposing the thinness of the veneer of civilization.

As Hardy noted in his diary, apparently in 1881, "Consider the Wordsworthian dictum (the more perfectly the natural object is repro-duced, the more truly poetic the picture). This reproduction is achieved by seeing into the *heart of the thing* . . . and is realism. In fact, though through being pursued by means of the imagination it is confounded with inven-tion" (*LWTH*, p. 151). Here Hardy has it both ways. He is being "realistic" just by virtue of his imagination of things, which might look like invention but gets to the real truth of the matter. And the truth is the life that lies outside of mere convention.

Casterbridge itself, as Hardy imagines it, might even be taken as a figure for the aesthetic and naturalistic tensions I have been describing. Like Hardy's novels themselves, Casterbridge is geometrically constructed, "rectangular," a mosaic work, set in a world wilder and uncontrolled, "miles of rotund down and concave field." It takes the vision of a bird flying over the city and not stopping there to recognize what Casterbridge does to the landscape. It sees the shape, the human construction, that contrasts so sharply with the world around it. Its citizens, however, see only an "indistinct mass" (ch. 4, p. 23). Inside Casterbridge the 20-year hiatus in Henchard's life is played out. But the narrative begins outside – with the Henchards' trek on the dusty roads. The mythic extravagance of the wife sale, the very kernel of the novel's symmetrical plot, happens outside the formal, civilized frame of the city. And Henchard dies outside it. Self-banished he goes to die as far from human construction of the city as possible, so far that Farfrae and Elizabeth-Jane give up their search for him.

They get their last trace of Henchard in that distant place, where he dies: Abel Whittle's decaying cottage, "of humble dwellings surely the humblest." Its walls are crumbling back into nature, "worn by years of rain-washings . . . channeled and sunken from its plane, its gray rents held together here and there by a leafy strap of ivy . . . Leaves from the fence had been blown into the corners of the doorway" (ch. 45, p. 250). The natural world reaffirms itself outside Casterbridge, in the completion of Henchard's life, almost like the "garden" in T. H. Huxley's "Prolegomena" to *Evolution and Ethics*. There Huxley imagines a metaphorical garden, formally enclosed against the cosmic processes of nature. It can be sustained successfully only by rigorous and ruthless culling by virtually authoritarian leadership, but in the end, Nature reasserts itself against the geometric protections of the human garden, and the geometric history of Henchard. It is art that makes life possible – the city rectangular like the novels; what lies beyond art can only be intimated by art, but what lies beyond art completes, one might say even makes, the story.

II

The Mayor of Casterbridge plays out in the character of Henchard and the form of tragedy the fundamental struggle in Hardy between a recognition of and a commitment to forces of nature that are both brutally indifferent and wonderfully vital and strategies of protection not only from those forces but also from the society that imposes false order upon them. The apparent disorder of nature yields to the ordering power of art.

Henchard begins trudging wearily out of a realist novel, longing for a freedom that one of the primary instruments in human efforts to contain nature – marriage – prevents. His story is largely of the price that must be paid for the powers of irrational energy that manifest themselves in desire. But they are also of the price of not fully honoring the commitment, for Henchard irregularly bursts from the constraints of convention, as he does when he sells his wife in the first chapters, and then erratically strives to be conventional again, neither living completely with his daring and outlaw self nor comfortably with his conventional one. But even his determination to avoid excess is excessive, as in his 20-year vow of teetotaling austerity. The story both dramatizes the dangers that lie beyond the convention and evokes admiration for the irrational urgings of desire. It affirms the dignity of human will against the ultimate terror of a world inimical to intelligence, casually destructive, and inaccessible to the very language by which humanity designates it. The ordering of that wild nature is a kind of narrative "violence" but the violence of art is Hardy's best protection from the nature that awes and inspires him, that emerges persistently in his understories, and allows him his strategic affirmation of imagination and human will.

No one knew better than Hardy what Northrop Frye claimed about realism: "The realistic writer soon finds that the requirements of literary form and plausible content always fight against each other."[9] The nature that Darwin described and that Hardy inhabited would not yield to the demands of art. In translating experience into a meaning not inherent in the nature he so powerfully describes, Hardy becomes the figure that Lawrence imagined him to be – that is, a writer who confronts the irrational order (or disorder) of the natural world but who, in Victorian mode, backs away from the irrationalist, sensual, vital consequences of that confrontation. Henchard is at times admirably risk-taking, sincere in his passions, and always subject to irrational energies, but it is, after all, the cautious and wisely conventional Elizabeth-Jane who has the last word. And the book hangs ambivalently between.

The Mayor of Casterbridge threatens plausibility right from the start and is throughout an aggressively manipulated narrative. It is one of those remarkable Hardyesque achievements that manage to carry overwhelming conviction while, at every instance, tempting us to dismiss them as incredible. Despite its firm realist grounding in a recognizable agricultural context, *The Mayor of Casterbridge* moves with the texture of romance, through the space of dream and desire, yet ironically, as in more frankly romantic fictions, *Frankenstein* and *Wuthering Heights*, the space is startlingly symmetrical.[10] As against the sprawling three-decker and serial realist fiction that dominated the Victorian marketplace, these fictions focus intensely around a single consciousness and absorb the world into that consciousness's needs. Novels as different from Hardy's as possible, like Jane Austen's *Northanger Abbey* (1818), or Charlotte Bronte's *Jane Eyre* (1848), or Charles Dickens's *Great Expectations* (1859), belong to that romance tradition in which the narrative seems to be shaped to answer to the protagonist's desires, or reflect in all its characters and actions the protagonist's feelings. Everything in the novel's world reflects the protagonist or refers to him.

These narratives, demonstrating the folly of great expectations and the moral disaster of imposing the self on experience, blur the distinction between the self and other. The protagonist's fate is somehow entirely created by the self. It is not at all simply wish fulfillment, not at all simply that Jane Eyre gets the man she loves, but, rather, that she gets the conditions in which she actually lives by virtue of qualities intrinsic to herself. In that tradition, Henchard's desires – even of self-obliteration – create the conditions in which he lives.

In such novels, plot bears the burden of uncommonness, and in *The Mayor of Casterbridge*, Hardy is consistent with his own dictum that the unreality should be in plot rather than in "character." But plot is not merely a vehicle for the display of "character." In effect it might be taken *as* character: it is the means through which Hardy both animates his world and imposes a structure on it. The world of *The Mayor of Casterbridge* corresponds, if only in a perverse and upside-down way, to Henchard's character. In the first half, it responds to Henchard's desire; in the second half it absolutely rejects it. If Henchard wants a sunny day for the fair, it will rain. One feels in the plot a mysterious but irresistible power lying behind the beautifully observed quotidian and asserting itself against the will of the protagonist in such a way as to imply a dramatic, if uneven, contest. One feels it despite the simple and abstract assertion of Hardy's pessimism, as in the narrator's invocation of the "ingenious machinery contrived by the Gods for reducing human possibilities of amelioration to a minimum" (ch. 44, p. 241). It is the Hardy who gives us little Father Time, and precisely not the Hardy whose engagement with the natural world implies a feeling for life even in the midst of bitter recognition of nature's overwhelming indifference. The language Hardy uses in his darkest passages, very often in fact, goes far beyond "indifference" to locate some positive malice – "ingenious machinery" – in the workings of the world. The plot of *The Mayor of Casterbridge*, like the world Hardy philosophizes, twists toward disaster but even in that twisting implies a meaningful – if perverse – world, which is further complicated by the recognition that the external ferocity is inherent in the human will itself. But the dark romantic intensity implies as well resistance to the disorder and meaninglessness it threatens. The effect is achieved particularly by Hardy's relish for the "uncommon," his insistence on facing up to the most extreme possibilities.

In the numbing sequence of misfortunes that befall Henchard, none is minimized. They exist not in an aura of nostalgia for intensities no longer available to the disenchanted narrator in the grey modern world, but as continuing realities that no wisdom can efface. "A Story of a Man of Character," as the subtitle has it, announces precisely the sort of character who would find realist disenchantment and compromise unendurable. In the first chapter, he astonishingly casts it off. Henchard moves in a landscape of ancient ruins, cornfields, Egdon Heath, all governed by the inexorable repetitions and transformations of time, all threatening to absorb him: yet in this landscape Henchard asserts his specialness; he refuses to acquiesce in compromise with the forces that require that he diminish his claims and make his peace. He outwits both society and nature by anticipating the worst they can do, and he leaves his last testament, his _will_, to assert his final contradictory power.

Against the extravagance of Henchard's plot, there is a realist's parallel plot – plausible, moderate, compromised. Farfrae serves as the realist protagonist, who has no passionate intensity. He is a protagonist out of a mid-Victorian novel, seen, however, from a new perspective: he makes moderate demands, he is quietly self-interested, resistant to excess, incapable of the kind of overbearing but passionate friendship that Henchard feels. His amiable shallowness is first observed in his moving rendition of "It's hame, and it's hame, hame fain would I be, O hame, hame, hame to my ain countree." This is followed by his announcement that he is going to "foreign parts" (ch. 8, p. 41).

Tested against this compromised realist hero, the overreaching Henchard emerges as by far more admirable, if less amiable. When, at the end, Elizabeth-Jane attempts to enlist Farfrae in a search for the wandering Henchard, Farfrae has no objections: "Although Farfrae had never so passionately liked Henchard as Henchard liked him, he had, on the other hand, never so passionately hated in the same direction as his former friend had done; and he was therefore not the least indisposed to assist Elizabeth-Jane in the laudable plan" (ch. 45, p. 248). It is part of the peculiarly Hardyesque work of the novel that Farfrae, achieving a life of compromise and social charm, stands finally in the landscape of Casterbridge successful within the terms of traditional Victorian realism but humanly diminished before Henchard's grand disasters. Henchard's story and Farfrae's comment almost parodically on each other. In his reversal of the comic pattern that tended to inform earlier Victorian realist fiction, Hardy in effect rejects the tradition of Victorian compromise, which he seems to have regarded as the mode of Laodicean moderation. Farfrae lives happily ever after with a self-conscious moderate Elizabeth-Jane, and Henchard, having loved and hated and acted spontaneously and aspired to more than nature itself could satisfy, gives up on life, but in a way that ironically seems an affirmation of the excessive will that led him to his successes and his doom.

Hardy's violation of the conventions of realism does not free his narrative for the creative unions of romance or challenging of the gods, but leads to the very defeat from which, one might have thought, the romantic rejection of realism would have protected it. Even here, Hardy plays with realism's conventions; for it was certainly a part – if an impure part – of the conventions of Victorian realism that manipulations of plot (Dickensian coincidences are only extreme examples) enact for the protagonists the desires hindered by the particularities and complexities of experience. Victorian fiction is dominated by the providential plot, in which turns of fate lead the protagonists toward the long-delayed and even sometimes unlikely comic ending, resolution, and marriage. While the Victorian realist must unrealistically use coincidence to resolve narratives, Hardy implies that the most realistic use of coincidence is not comic conjunction but tragic disruption. The world simply isn't made to confirm our desires. There is no justice or mercy built into nature. All the more reason that so radically flawed a protagonist as Henchard evokes the admiration of writers like Lawrence and Woolf – taking the risk of desire is a heroic act.

Coincidence provides the chance event that explodes the fantasy of happiness. Although Elizabeth-Jane must renounce the enthusiasm that made Henchard so much "a man of character," she continues to wonder "at the persistence of the unforeseen" (ch. 45, p. 252). Everything in the novel points to the exceptional nature, not of disaster, but of the "tranquility" she seeks; what predominates in life is the "unforeseen and injustice." In Elizabeth-Jane it is not shallowness, as it is with Farfrae, that makes for survival. Although she is one of the lucky ones, she *knows* she is lucky. Having had more passion to begin with, she knows the price of tranquility, as Farfrae does not.

Despite Elizabeth-Jane's concluding voice, *The Mayor of Casterbridge* is almost a celebration of disaster. Willingness to dare it and power to shape it become Henchard's dignity. He chooses his own disaster, down to his last moments, when, with the possibility of a new beginning before him, we learn that "he had no … desire" (ch. 41, p. 291). The limiting of desire, a condition for survival in a nature incompatible with human feeling, is also a surrender to death. Henchard becomes an inverted romantic hero: he makes his own fate. *The Mayor of Casterbridge*, while dramatizing man's contingent and compromised nature, imagines the possibility of something freer. It pushes beyond the "small solicitation of circumstance" (*Middemarch*, ch. 89, p. 771) that George Eliot's realism dramatized as the real evil, to a celebration of democratic human energies that Victorian realism had so often determined to repress.

Critics have long recognized that Henchard, in one way or another, *is* the world of *The Mayor of Casterbridge*. Like Frankenstein before him, he absorbs all external reality into his dream of the self. Technically, this means not only that every character and event in the novel relates directly to Henchard, but that the more carefully one examines the novel, the more evident it is that other characters reflect aspects of his enormous selfhood. As Victor Frankenstein can be recognized as his monster's double, but also Clerval's, his mother's, his brother's, Walton's, so Henchard can be seen as the double of Farfrae and Elizabeth-Jane, Jopp and Abel Whittle, Newson and Lucetta. As Victor moves with erratic repetitiveness from act to reaction, from aspiration to repentance, so Henchard enacts his self-division and Hardy projects that division on the landscape of his narrative. It is all done with the recklessness of conventional plausibility that marks gothic conventions, and yet it achieves a new sort of plausibility. For the large techniques of romance are incorporated here into the texture of realism that allows every monstrous quirk its credible place in a social, historical, and geographical context. The landscape of the self in this novel almost displaces the landscape of that hard, unaccommodating actual to the representation of which the realist has always been dedicated. But self and other exist here in a delicate balance, and it is probably more appropriate to say that in *The Mayor of Casterbridge* Hardy makes overt the continuing and inevitable presence of romance in all realistic fiction. What Lawrence detects as vital energy amid rigid social conventions, Hardy embodies in a protagonist that he cannot allow to survive but cannot help admiring.

We may take the remarkable first scene, in which Henchard sells his wife, as a perfect example of the narrative modes of the mature Hardy, whose qualities I have been discussing. His writing in style and substance embodies the tensions between the conventions of realism and those of romance. And these in turn reflect the tensions between his fear of losing his respectability and his continuing fascination with the human energies that transcend social convention. In the midst of a meticulous but perhaps too professorial prose, he daringly represents the uncommon in the common. He suffuses the realist landscape with an almost mythic force; attention to detail carries with it some aura of meaning not quite captured, of large energies lurking beneath the surface and of big events to come. The whole sequence confronts directly the problem of inventing satisfying ways to cope with the limiting pressures of the realist's contingent world on large human energies and aspiration. Here Hardy exploits the conventions of realism to free himself from bondage to the conventional real. He takes the risk of alienating readers by a narrative extravagance – the selling of Henchard's wife – that echoes in its daring great tragedy, like *King Lear*, but that also violates in a radical way ideals not only of propriety but of simple moral decency. His daring is morally dubious, but it implies both a new freedom of imagination and a new pre-Lawrentian conception of human dignity. The freedom and the dignity are precisely in the willingness to take the risk. It is not only Henchard who takes the risk, but it is Hardy the writer and artist moving outside moral and aesthetic norms of realism.

The voice is that of Hardy's distant narrator. While he is close enough to observe the most minute details of the scene and the characters, his voice sounds from afar, and seems only to know the surfaces. As Henchard and his wife walk through "the thick hoar of dust" (ch. 1, p. 5) that dims their shoes and all their clothing, their gestures, not their described thoughts, reveal the internal drama. Darwin's strategy of seeking traces that will reveal history is the strategy of Hardy's prose here, and for the most part throughout all his novels. Realism's attention to descriptive detail is Hardy's chosen mode. The intense care to register what can be observed precisely is almost awkward. "At his back he carried by a looped rope a rush basket, from which protruded at one end the crutch of a hay-knife, a wimble for hay-bonds being also visible in the aperture" (ch. 1, p. 5). This not only identifies the walker's trade, but also identifies the narrator as one who looks carefully and knows a great deal about agricultural work. The narrator reads not only the tools but also the bearing of the man – he has a "springless walk" which is to be distinguished from "the desultory shamble of the general laborer" (ch. 1, p. 5). The traces accumulate, and the visible man begins to have a character and a history, but never because the

narrator simply tells us what they are. He tells us, instead, how the man
looks, as though he, like the readers themselves, is trying to figure it out. He
has no more access to the inner Henchard than we do. The psychology, as
is typical for Hardy, is played out in the action.

Strikingly, that action begins in more than disenchantment, in utter
fatigue with the Victorian realist's happy ending – marriage. By the time
we meet the still-young Henchard, he has been married for some time, and
there is no romance left. Henchard himself is described as a man of "fine
figure, swarthy, and stern in aspect; and he showed in profile a facial angle
so slightly inclined as to be almost perpendicular" (ch. 1, p. 5).
The language struggles to place the characters and define them against
recognizable nonliterary categories. "What was really peculiar" about the
couple, something even an observer less keen than the narrator would have
noted, "was the perfect silence they observed" (ch. 1, p. 5). Here is marriage:
the ideal of the hearth, of the limited but satisfying life to which Dickens
led his protagonists, in which Adam Bede resolves his career, has turned
bitter. Look closely. What "from afar" might be taken as "easy confidential
chat of people full of reciprocity" becomes "on closer view" avoidance – the
"taciturnity unbroken." "That the man and the woman were husband and
wife . . . there could be little doubt. No other than such relationship could
have accounted for the stale familiarity which [they] carried along with
them like a nimbus as they moved down the road" (ch. 1, p. 6). One of the
significant measures of Victorian realism's turn away from comic form is its
gradualist treatment of the way marriages break down. Hardy, however,
takes the long painful process as a given and begins with marriage as already
disappointment and imprisonment. Such an understanding should cast
a shadow over the book's happy ending – Farfrae and Elizabeth-Jane
together for life.

Later, with the realist's detailed, analytic, inferential style he describes
the furmity tent: "At the upper end stood a stove, containing a charcoal
fire, over which hung a large three-legged crock, sufficiently polished
round the rim to show that it was made of bell metal" (ch. 1, p. 8). In all
cases, the narrator remains learnedly distant, not emotionally engaged with
the events, but wise and perceptive and determined to see with objectivity
and precision. The narrator's distance, however, is not quite total. Without
entering the minds of his characters, he implies familiarity with their ways:
"there was more in that tent than met the cursory glance, and the man,
with the instinct of a perverse character, sensed it quickly" (ch. 1, p. 8).
The texture of the language implies that the objective narrator is also
worldly-wise, has heard and repeated a thousand such untold stories, and

is capable of telling tales that are yet somehow relevant to the realities of our own day.

The quality of "tale" is reinforced as the drunken Henchard, with embittered irony, announces, "I am open to an offer for this gem of creation" (ch. 1, p. 10), that is, for Susan, his wife. The dreary realism of the opening descriptions issues into a world of myth and tragedy; the myth is to be taken as literally credible: "It has been done elsewhere," says Henchard (in Hardy's bid to hang on to realist credibility), "and why not here?" (ch. 1, p. 12).

Just as the scene bursts the limits of the conventions of realism, and daringly requires comparison to the abrupt beginning of *King Lear*, so Henchard attempts to free himself from the limiting conditions of his life. Describing a drunken, disillusioned binder of sheaves, Hardy does not move to the manner of naturalist realism. The style sustains that texture of myth and distance even as the dense particularity suggests that Henchard has been diminished by his dusty, socially constrained context; the sullenness of his relation to a wife, who has herself been ground down by "civilization"; the "stale familiarity" (ch. 1, p. 6) of their relationship; and the "dogged and cynical indifference" (ch. 1, p. 5) manifest in every movement and feature of the man. As we meet him plodding beside his wife, Henchard is (significantly) pretending to read a ballad sheet, turning from the reality of his intimacy with her to a poet's dream of the uncommon. As he drinks, this partly defeated man is transformed, rising to "serenity," then becoming "jovial," then "argumentative," and finally "the qualities signified by the shape of his face, the occasional clench of his mouth, and the fiery spark of his dark eye, begin to tell in his conduct; he was overbearing ... even brilliantly quarrelsome" (ch. 1, p. 9). The latent Henchard, released only partly by alcohol from the restrictions of convention and responsibility, becomes realized. He asserts the sense of his own power and longs to be free to exercise it: "I'd challenge England to beat me in the fodder business; and if I were a free man again, I'd be worth a thousand pound before I'd done 't" (ch. 1, p. 9).

Against the conventions of the realism that Hardy is putting behind him, Henchard pushes his fantasy to the point of making it real. The larger wish becomes father to the fact, and the realistically created scene slides into romance in which Henchard is hero. Within a few pages, by a process the reader is not allowed to observe, Henchard has become mayor of Casterbridge – the drunken fantasy becomes the premise of the entire novel. Ironically, the action that violates all conventions turns Henchard into an eminently respectable man. But he is clearly a man who, however firmly his will keeps him under control (as it keeps him from drinking for 21 years), acts outside the limits that confine ordinary people. He threatens to become a Lawrentian figure, and it is certainly this potentiality that evokes Lawrence's admiration.

Henchard seems able to withstand the pressures that impinge on other lives, yet all of his life in reality curls around the monstrous secret of the sale of his wife. As Frankenstein hides from his monster, attempts to rejoin the community and conceal his great dream and his great mistake, so Henchard hides from the reality so vividly and abruptly rendered in the first scene. All of the novel grows from the narrative of the inevitable reemergence of that hidden fact, that illicit thrust at "freedom," into the community in which Henchard seeks to find his peace. But his mayorship is only a disguised reenactment of the forbidden scene. In Casterbridge, Henchard seeks to assert the absolute power of his self over a constricting and contingent world. At the level of myth he plays out the story that Hardy tells in almost every one of his novels, with the same ambivalence: the quest for respectability and status at the price of disguising not only lower-class origins but also the "ape and the tiger."

Inevitably, with the rhythms of myth and the details of modern realism, the pressures Henchard denied at the start avenge themselves on him, and with a completeness far beyond what the logic of his situation would require. But once set in a world carefully defined in the language of social analysis and historical tradition, once seen in the context of delicate financial and human transactions, Henchard must be destroyed. The man of large feeling and deep need – the hero of romance – cannot survive in the context of a carefully particularized society. Henchard is incapable of suppressing, at least for long, his powerful, desiring self. Neither success nor failure can be ordinary for him. And since the conventions the novel adopts make failure the only possibility for the largely aspiring man, it must be an extraordinary failure. The novel concentrates on the losses, juxtaposes his large ambition to the moderate ones of Farfrae, and conspires to keep him from the comforts of the real. Henchard is his fate, and the narrative line transcends the limits of realism by cooperating with Henchard's refusal to compromise. All coincidences conspire to make things worse than the compromising conditions of realism would demand.

But they are not coincidences; they are Henchard writ large. The usual extravagances of Hardy's plotting here serve to produce a strange coherence – not so much realist credibility, but aesthetically consistent form and mood. Henchard's domination of the book, uncharacteristic of Hardy's work as a whole, implies his hand – or spirit – everywhere. His domination implies the force of irrational – and yet artistically comprehensible – energy that underlies the material surfaces of Hardy's world. Henchard evokes all the characters whose coincidental appearance plays so important a part in the novel, and with each of these, at some point, he reverses roles. In the third chapter, for example, we learn of Susan and Elizabeth-Jane's search for Henchard, which brings them to Casterbridge and reopens his past; not long before we hear of Henchard's search for them, itself significantly cut short by "a certain shyness of revealing his conduct" (ch. 2, p. 17). Again, Henchard is responsible for persuading Farfrae, who will end the novel as the new mayor of Casterbridge, to remain in the town. Later, Lucetta, who had nursed him in an illness, arrives in order to marry Henchard, and he must repay her kindness and reverse their early relationship. The furmity woman comes to town to expose him and, in the strong scene in which she is brought to trial before him, she argues, "he's no better than I, and has no right to sit there in judgment upon me." Henchard agrees, "I'm no better than she" (ch. 28, p. 154). Even Jopp, who is responsible for the information leading to the skimmity ride, arrives in town just after Farfrae to take the job that Henchard has offered to Farfrae; by the end, Henchard is living where Jopp lives. Henchard creates the world which is to destroy him – even becomes that world.

The force of the idea that, as Hardy quotes Novalis, "character is fate" (ch. 17, p. 89), is worked out with a minuteness that ironically seems to translate the whole world of the novel, so carefully without analysis of the inner lives of the characters, into a psychic landscape. Farfrae's dramatic entrance into the novel, for example, corresponds precisely to the moment when, defending himself against a popular demand that he replace the bad wheat he has sold, Henchard says, "If anybody will tell me how to turn grown wheat into wholesome wheat, I'll take it back with pleasure. But it can't be done" (ch. 5, p. 31). Farfrae arrives and does it. Farfrae only remains in the novel because of Henchard's overwhelming emotional demands on him: "It's providence!" Farfrae says, "should anyone go against it?" (ch. 9, p. 51). Henchard makes providence.

More important for a full sense of the daring of Hardy's achievement is the way he takes pains to call attention to the creaking mechanics of his novel. It is as though Hardy wants to make sure that we do notice how remarkable, unlikely, or chancy an event has been. When Farfrae turns up, the narrator remarks, "He might possibly have passed without stopping at all, or at most for half a minute to glance in at the scene, had not his advent coincided with the discussion on corn and bread; in which event this history had never been enacted" (ch. 6, p. 31). Here Hardy turns what might well have been taken as a donnée of the plot into a coincidence upon which the whole plot must turn. Coincidence in story implies narrative purposefulness. Coincidence here makes manifest Henchard's responsibility for his own fate. As the story unfolds, Henchard's impulsive energy can be seen to be responsible for every stage of his eventual self-obliteration. He too impulsively reveals his past to Farfrae; he too severely punishes Abel Whittle; he too ambitiously tries to outdo Farfrae in setting up a fair for the holidays; he too hastily dismisses Farfrae and too angrily responds to Farfrae's determination to set up his own business; he cuts off the courtship between Farfrae and Elizabeth-Jane, although, as the narrator remarks, "one would have supposed Henchard to have had policy to see that no better *modus vivendi* could be arrived at with Farfrae than by encouraging him to become his son-in-law" (ch. 17, p. 88). Later he too hastily buys corn and then far too hastily sells it. He opens Susan's letter about Elizabeth-Jane at precisely that moment when being recognized as Elizabeth-Jane's father, "the act he had prefigured for weeks with a thrill of pleasure," was to become "no less than a miserable insipidity … His reinstation of her mother "had been chiefly for the girl's sake, and the fruition of the whole scheme was such dust and ashes as this" (ch. 19, p. 99).

The novel even implies that it is Henchard's responsibility that Susan dies. After reading a letter from Lucetta, Henchard says, "Upon my heart and soul, if ever I should be left in a position to carry out that marriage with thee, I *ought* to do it, indeed!" The narrator comments, "The contingency he had in mind was, of course, the death of Mrs. Henchard" (ch. 18, p. 91). And the narrative immediately records the death of Mrs. Henchard. Every detail of the action feeds into Henchard's being, and every detail of the text requires that we accept it only if we are willing to accept the extravagant with the plausible, or as part of it.

In Hardy, the plot makes the real mythic. The myth that Hardy creates here does not in any way adumbrate a universe in which moral order has any significance. It works with a mindless indifference that has no lessons for humans. It is far more about energy and life and death than about justice, although it might be possible to read into Henchard's downfall a nemesis of the sort that often makes for poetic justice in Victorian realist fiction and that remains implicit even in George Eliot's self-consciously secular narratives. Henchard's tragedy is not about justice or nemesis. The pattern is similar, but what matters here, almost exclusively, is not constrained by moral assumptions and conventions. It is the self. It is Henchard himself. Henchard, the tragic king, responsible both for his kingdom and the sin that blights its wheat and him, must move with ironic absoluteness to death, not because he is punished for his sins, but because he has, self-consciously or not, let his vital energy direct his actions. But also because he is a man of indecision. In both guises, he acts outside the rational norms of the society he both dominates and loses.

The movement toward death is prefigured early. "Why the deuce did I come here!" Henchard asks, as he finds himself in the place of public execution after discovering, because of his refusal to heed the instructions on the envelope, that Elizabeth-Jane is not his daughter (ch. 20, p. 98). "The momentum of his character knew no patience," the narrator later remarks (ch. 27, p. 145). That momentum moves him past all possibility of compromise, to disaster. He is saved from suicide after the skimmity ride only by the magical appearance of his effigy in the water. When the furmity woman returns, Henchard has no instinct toward the deception that would allow him to keep his long-held secret quiet. By attempting to kill Farfrae he not only finally alienates the last man who might save him, but makes it impossible for Farfrae to believe him when he attempts to inform Farfrae of Lucetta's illness. Again, his relation to Farfrae is rather like Oedipus's relation to the careful Creon. Thus, since he carelessly gave Jopp Lucetta's letters, he is responsible for Lucetta's death in two ways.

His last two self-assertive acts complete his self-annihilation. He breaks into the royal visit, demanding the recognition that he had lost and forcing his first scuffle with Farfrae. And when Newson returns to claim Elizabeth-Jane, Henchard unhesitatingly (driven by impulses similar to those that led him to sell his wife) asserts that she is dead; his final act of deceit loses for him his last possibility of survival within the community. The narrative takes on the quality of a pagan ritual of self-annihilation. He refuses to plead for himself to Elizabeth-Jane: "Among the many hindrances to such a pleading not the least was this, that he did not sufficiently value himself to lessen his sufferings by strenuous effort or elaborate argument" (ch. 44, p. 246). Elizabeth-Jane discovers that "it was part of his nature to extenuate nothing, and I live on as one of his own worst accusers" (ch. 45, p. 248). She then goes out to look for him. To the last, the power of his being draws people after him. Elizabeth-Jane and Farfrae seek him; Abel Whittle, against Henchard's command, follows him, and aids him as he can. Henchard walks until he can walk no more and ends in a hovel (the whole scene deliberately and daringly constructed to recall King Lear and Edgar in the storm). In writing his will, he wills his total obliteration:

MICHAEL HENCHARD'S WILL
That Elizabeth-Jane be not told of my death, or
   made to grieve on account of me
"&that I be not bury'd in consecrated ground.
"&that no sexton be asked to toll the bell.
"&that nobody is wished to see my dead body.
"&that no murners walk behind me at my funeral
"&no flours be planted on my grave,
"&that no man remember me.
"to this I put my name. MICHAEL HENCHARD.   (ch. 45, p. 289)

Plainly, absolutely assertive as it is, the will's ambivalence emerges with
tragic force. It is in a "will" that Henchard denies himself. He obliterates
himself in capital letters. His last written words are the name he is asking to
obliterate. In death itself he asserts the dominance of his name. Henchard
becomes here the absolute self of the fiction he created of his life and of the
world. He ends, like the late-century writers who had, in effect, given up on
the ideals of Victorian writers who spoke to their audiences in effort to
move the world. Since he cannot transform the ideal into the real, he
transforms the real into the ideal. It is, as we shall see, the method of
Hardy's art itself.

In the last chapters, the narrator quietly extends the sort of ironic
critique of Farfrae, that figure of conventional social success, that is implied
in the affirmation of Henchard's dominance. Everywhere, Farfrae acts so as
to represent a practical alternative to Henchard's egoist passion for the
absolute. The final complex of alternatives and doublings comes when
Henchard arrives at the wedding feast, like the ancient mariner, an unin-
vited guest with a monstrous tale he might tell. But he is mute, and hears
instead Donald's voice "giving strong expression to a song of his dear native
country that he loved so well as never to have revisited" (ch. 44, p. 244).
And yet here is Henchard, actually "revisiting" his home, although he had
intended to flee it forever. It is Henchard, not Farfrae, who sentimentally
leaves the canary, and it is at this point that Farfrae is described as "not the
least indisposed" to try to find Henchard, largely because, like a good
Laodicean, he has never cared enough either to hate or to love him. For
a moment, that is, Hardy ironically rejects an art (and its avatar, Farfrae)
that drains energy from experience and settles for the rules of common
sense and the inevitable contingencies of ordinary life.

The last word of the novel belongs to Elizabeth-Jane, a figure who does
not fit easily into any of the patterns discussed here. She seems at home in
the world of realistic conventions that Henchard's narrative implicitly

mocks. Elizabeth-Jane provides the only other perspective from which we see a large part of the experience. Although she never surrenders to her impulses or to her needs, she is not simply a Farfrae. Herself entangled in respectability, Elizabeth-Jane becomes the most authentic commentator on Henchard's experience. Her heart remains always in hiding. It stirs momentarily for Henchard's grand misguided attempts at mastery. But in her submission to the movements of the novel's narrative, she becomes an expression of the way in which "happiness was but the occasional episode in a general drama of pain" (p. 290). By accepting this view, staying protected within the limits of respectability, and not rejoicing too much when good fortune comes, she survives to find "tranquility" and to forget the Henchard whose death brought her vision. She is the best surrogate for the realist's audience as it watches a tragic drama. She is where the promethean Hardy hides.

Her preoccupation with respectability indicates her acceptance of the limits society imposes on action and on dreams, but with her, the acceptance is an act of self-protection. There is something in Elizabeth-Jane of Hardy's own tentativeness, for while, in Henchard, Hardy ambitiously projects the passions of a large ego beyond the limits of conventional fiction, the narrative voice in which he tells the story has something of Elizabeth-Jane's own reserve, and of the wisdom she has achieved by the end of the novel. Henchard is Hardy's fantasy of liberation, of freed desire. Elizabeth-Jane enacts a dignified and understandable retreat, a return to the conventions of realism with a new understanding of the stakes. She is a strong reminder, even as she fills the role of the woman who marries and makes for the happy ending of Victorian realist novels, that the world really doesn't shape itself morally, that it is not accessible to the commonsense structures and language of earlier realists, that behind the veneer of society and the quiet movement of ordinary life there lies the "unforeseen," the continuing pain, the irrational intensities of nature and human nature.

In effect, she articulates the ideology of Victorian realism, in a novel with Lawrentian aspirations to authenticity of natural being. She has learned, and she teaches, "The secret ... of making limited opportunities by a species of microscopic treatment, of those minute forms of satisfaction that offer themselves to everybody not in positive pain" (ch. 45, p. 252). It is Apollonian, not Dionysian. It is where Hardy hides as he secretly affirms the vital energies that are the most singular and impressive aspects of his art, and whose dangers he could celebrate in hiding. The minute forms of nature – the ephemera that reappear unexpectedly from time to time and all that unperceived life that he registers in the midst of his most intense dramas – these are also aesthetically minute forms of satisfaction. In creating Henchard, Hardy almost avoids turning the "exceptional person" into the bad guy to be punished. He is punished anyway, but even in defeat he hangs on to the energy that has driven him there and affirms his name in capital letters as he dies; Elizabeth-Jane resists the Lawrentian and Promethean aspiration that makes her settling for minute forms of satisfaction look like cowardice.

Like Hardy, we can admire from a distance Henchard's Promethean qualities; but no more than Elizabeth-Jane herself could we have lived with them. While she is honorable and right when she sensibly (and realistically) follows Henchard's literal instructions on the grounds "that the man who wrote them meant what he said" (ch. 45, p. 250), the reader recalls that he had rarely done what he meant.

Formally shaped as it is, *The Mayor of Casterbridge* rarely lapses into philosophy. There is nothing tendentious about it: the drama counterpoints the two poles of Henchard's character: the one irrationally aspiring to freedom, power, and deep satisfaction of the self; the other symmetrically rebounding from acts of self-assertion into socially defensive reflexes and self-destructive actions. The art contains and gives form to both poles and the satisfactions it yields are not minute.

Interlude
Jude *and the Power of Art*

That combination of sensuous ambition and controlled artistry – compounded with extreme sensitivity both to natural phenomena and social convention – a combination that marks *the Mayor of Casterbridge* in particular – gives to Hardy's works their distinctive quality. In particular, it distinguishes his novels from the contemporary efflorescence of literary naturalism, that most disenchanted of literary genres. Despite obvious affinities – Hardy's absorption of Darwinian ideas, his persistent emphasis on the indifference of nature, his persistent dramatization of the suffering both nature and society inflict on those who are not privileged (and a few who are) – Hardy resisted even with revulsion literary naturalism. It was not mere prissiness or defensiveness that led him to say to Frances Henniker, in response to the violence of the attacks on his later works, that

> You mistake in supposing that I admire Zola. It is just what I don't do. *I think him no artist*, and too material, I feel that the animal side of human nature should never be dwelt on except as contrast to its spiritual side. (*CL*, II, 157)

Hardy's emphasis on "the spiritual side" of human nature, something distinct from and at war with the animal, marks also his difference from Lawrence. Lawrence was wary of the "spiritual" since for him the physical and the spiritual were one; he believed that the only real spirituality was in and through the body. For Hardy, however, as for so many of his Victorian contemporaries, not least the scientific naturalists like T. H. Huxley and John Tyndall, the presence of the spiritual in the material was an unresolvable paradox: body and soul are both steadily opposed and mutually dependent. It is just the fact of their being mixed that most pains Hardy and that most disturbs his protagonists. While Hardy is insistent that the merely material does not represent the truth of things, he regularly dramatizes how the ideal distorts and undervalues the bodily.

73

But the critical point in his rejection of French naturalism is in the phrase I have italicized: "I think him no artist." In one of the entries made in his "biography," Hardy insists that "'realism' is not Art." For Art is a distortion that "brings out more forcibly than might otherwise be done that feature in them which appeals most strongly to the idiosyncrasy of the artist" (*LW*, p. 239). At one point he claims that "if I were a painter I would paint a picture of a room as viewed by a mouse from a chink under the skirting" (*LW*, p. 246). Art gives shape and meaning to the material. Meaning lies in the perspective, in the conscious position of the viewer, not in the thing itself. Here another great Hardyan paradox kicks in: the ideal is essential to meaning and order; the material is incompatible with the ideal. It is the work of the artist to overcome the paradox.

Hardy is always self-conscious about the "art" of his work. His concern with the ideal as his characters conceive it complicates his commitment to be truthful in representation of the material. Particularly in *A Pair of Blue Eyes*, and later in *Tess*, as we have seen, this tension between ideal and lived reality becomes the dramatic center of the narrative. In those books but perhaps less obviously in others, he dramatizes the disasters entailed in idealizing. But this dramatization is contained within meticulously constructed narratives that resist with their symmetries, their ironies, their careful juxtapositions, the chaos of indifferent materiality. In his last two novels, *Jude the Obscure* and *The Well-Beloved*, he pushes to painful, even incredible, extremes his exploration of the relation between material and ideal.

Throughout, Hardy remained the self-conscious artist. He shared certain attitudes that he recognized in Zola, and was as evasive as he had to be to keep from being seen, as were the French naturalists, as not respectable; his lifetime preference for poetry over the fiction that made his reputation and his wealth was a symptom of his constant concern for "art." His claim that Zola was not an artist was no mere cover-up of his uneasiness about being seen as merely "material" and "sensuous," a libidinous and lewd writer. While his books may be thematic cousins to the work of the French naturalists, he insisted, justly enough, that they are otherwise not related. They are utterly different in structure, overall orientation, and feeling for the material world. As I have been arguing, despite their thematic darkness, Hardy's novels retain an aura of enchantment, even as he draws with meticulous precision the texture of the harshly indifferent natural world. That world, operating outside the limits of the protagonists' interests and desire, emerges as a vital and usually beautiful understory to the dark stories of defeat and disaster. The books, as they move to inevitable tragedy, make beautiful patterns and derive their meaning from the strategies of art.

Hardy wanted to write novels and poems that were "more truthful than truth."[11] We have already seen how regularly his extraordinary registrations of the nuances of the natural world reverberate with a vitality that belies the darkness of his themes. Naturalist writing, he clearly believed, was not truer than true. It offended his nervous sensibilities but worse than that, it neither evoked nor implied any adequate sense of the ideal, nor was it adequately artful. Francis O'Gorman, emphasizing this aspect of Hardy's work, quotes him as saying, "the material is not the real – only the visible, the real being invisible optically." "The location of the real," says O'Gorman, "like the location of the ideal in *The Well-Beloved,* was not stable"; Hardy was always interested in "modes of perception, frames of observation."[12]

However consistent *Jude* may seem to be with the tragic darkness of Hardy's other late fiction, it is formally and aesthetically as anomalous as *The Well-Beloved.* Since discussion of *Jude* has required attention elsewhere, I will treat it here only briefly, with an eye to what it helps tell us about Hardy's views of art. Its affinity to the much less well-known *The Well-Beloved* will suggest how central to its conception and, indeed, to the energies that drive all of Hardy's work are these questions of the relation between material and ideal. In the next chapter, I will turn full attention to this problem as it becomes the thematic center of *The Well-Beloved.* But *Jude* is a radically disenchanted novel, with almost no context that will, as in other Hardy novels, re-enchant the difficult world. It takes to its limit the darkness of Hardy's vision, in part by being so austere and distant from Hardy's usual treatment of the natural world, and in part because its extravagant darkness smacks too often of the "philosophy" Hardy always denied drove his works. Ironically, the defeat in *The Well-Beloved* is more subtly handled, but implicitly more bitterly as well.

Virginia Woolf claims that *Jude* is the only one of Hardy's novels against which "we can fairly bring the charge of pessimism" (*VW*, p. 231). What she says of certain sentences in *Tess* might apply firmly to *Jude*: "The words protrude cold and raw, like the springs of a machine where we had seen only flesh and blood" (p. 231). "Done because we are too menny" has that raw extravagance about it – it is Malthus dressed up as a poor boy, little Father Time, an all-too-allegorical embodiment of Hardy's sense of modernity: "the coming universal wish not to live."

Jude may well be the most discussed of Hardy's novels, but it is certainly not the most representative, particularly in its exceptional austerity, its virtually unredeemed progress through a world where all beyond the human dramas tends to be reduced to starving crows, a trapped rabbit, and a stuck pig. What is artful in this ostensibly naturalistic narrative of doom? It is a perfect exemplar of the "tragedy" that Lawrence argues is at the center of all of Hardy's work: "the tragedy of those who, more or less pioneers, have died in the wilderness, whither they had escaped for free action, after having left the walled security, and the comparative imprisonment, of the established convention" (p. 411).

At the same time it becomes a perfect exemplar of that part of Hardy's art that Lawrence considered "rubbish." It is not merely the symmetrical opposed movement of the careers and attitudes of Jude and Sue. In the early pages he is a believer, she a free-spirited pagan; in the last pages he has lost belief while she is bound to the horror of fidelity to Christian doctrine. We have seen this kind of doubleness carried through to its tragic end in Henchard's fate in *The Mayor of Casterbridge*. From Lawrence's perspective, Hardy might be said to betray his art when he locks his characters inside convention, as Sue is repulsively locked in her marriage in the final pages. Instead of daring heroic resistance to convention, Hardy's characters succumb. Even in the daring *Mayor of Casterbridge*, the book does not come close to endorsing Henchard's "aristocratic" (as Lawrence would have it) rejection of convention at the moment he sells his wife. While Hardy allows his characters to resist, at least for a while, he will not allow the challenge to succeed. Like Henchard in his second thoughts, which reverse his emotionally charged, extravagant moves, Hardy shapes his novels under the pressure of second thoughts. The heavy price of such resistance is played out in their nemesis. While there is usually a struggle between the material and the ideal, between Jude's Greek New Testament and Arabella's "characteristic part of the pig," neither "Christminster" glowing in the distance nor "the well-beloved" is ever allowed life outside the dream of the protagonist. The ideal is a "seeming" and the quest must end badly.

Jude radically elaborates the old conflict between body and soul, and dramatizes the dangers of the body; while it works out the tragedy Lawrence describes, it does so in a way that makes the body the villain of the Agon. No other Hardy novel is so insistently preoccupied with the difference and the tension between mind and body, or so aware of their interplay. Jude's pilgrimage to Christminster begins and is sustained by extraordinary feats of self-denial, almost of disembodiment: "He had become entirely lost to his bodily situation" (Bk I, ch. 3, p. 63). Within the first pages of the novel, he loses contact with his body at least three times: when he allows the crows to eat in Farmer Troutham's fields (which leads, in turn, to *corporal* punishment), when he tries to observe the distant Christminster, and in the moments before he is struck "by a piece of flesh, the characteristic part of a barrow-pig" (Bk 1, ch. 6, p. 80).

Provoked by a hurting tooth, Hardy once wrote:

> I look in the glass. Am conscious of the humiliating sorriness of my earthly tabernacle, and of the sad fact that the best of parents could do no better for me . . . Why should a man's mind have been thrown into such close, sad, sensational, inexplicable relations with such a precarious object as his own body! (*LW*, p. 265)

Such tensions pervade the novel, every forgetfulness of flesh leading to its punishment (except for the entirely fleshly Arabella), every indulgence of flesh (for Jude and Sue, at least) leading to guilt and recriminations. The novel may conceive body and spirit as distinct and opposed elements, but they are always recognized as completely involved with each other. For Hardy this bodes disaster. In Lawrence, the quest for the fulfillment of the body is a kind of spiritual apotheosis; for Hardy, the indissolubility of mind and body subjects his protagonists to the inevitable limits of the merely physical, and makes impossible a fulfillment in which two incompatible parts of the same thing are required to become compatible. The division pushes *Jude* toward a schematic bleakness beyond realism, while at the same time persistent registration of mutual dependence anchors the narrative within the realist tradition of the mixed nature of things. At moments the actions are reduced to programmatic schemata, as when the narrator notes that Jude

> had singled [Arabella] out . . . as a woman is singled out in such cases, for no reasoned purpose of further acquaintance, but in commonplace obedience to conjunctive orders from headquarters, unconsciously received by unfortunate men when the last intention of their lives is to be occupied with the feminine. (Bk 1, ch. 6, p. 81)

Here the ironic circumlocutions emphasize the fundamental authority of the physical in language that, appropriately, disguises the raw physicality of human desire. This notorious crisis in *Jude*, diverting the hero from his quest for the ideal at Christminster, has, like so much else in this strained and frequently incredible narrative, something of the programmatic about it. The programmatic is assimilated to an overall formal project, manifest in the schematic nature of the book's entire structure.

There is no need here to linger in detail over the careful sets of parallels, juxtapositions, crossings, and bitter ironies that mark the narrative as a whole. But it is important to register at least generally how central is formal aesthetic harmony to Hardy's conception of the work (character-istic in this respect of most of Hardy's writing in fiction and poetry). If anything, the problem with *Jude* is not that it is naturalistically com-mitted to the full registration of the material details of the protagonists' lives, but that the "art" feels almost like "craft," too strict for the realist mode that Hardy ostensibly adopts. We will see how the extravagance of his usual mode is almost parodied in Jocelyn Pierston's infatuation with the ideal as it manifests itself in three generations of women. But in the long run, the story in *The Well-Beloved* is not much less credible than the story in *Jude*. Hardy's self-consciously structured narratives are nothing like the usually long, "scientific," literal representations of the naturalist novels of Zola. I am not interested here in an evaluative comparison, but only in pointing out that every step of the way in the progress of Hardy's protagonists is part of a clear design that works out relentlessly, even if against the grain of probability.

It is a commonplace that Jude and Sue trace opposite intellectual paths, that she begins enlightened and free spirited, Jude unenlightened and conservative; he moves toward disbelief and Sue returns to the constraints of piety. "My good heavens," Jude cries, "How we are changing places" (Part 6, ch. 3, p. 422). Then there are the gross juxtapositions. As against the Arabella passages, thick with flesh and carnality, in which Jude cannot begin to hope to sustain his intellectual interests and his pursuit of the ideal, there follow the Sue Bridehead passages. If Arabella is all flesh, Sue is a "disembodied creature" (Bk 4, ch. 5, p. 309). If at Marygreen Jude aspires to Oxford and is weighted down by carnality and sexuality, in Oxford he becomes a shade among shades, an invisible man. Body and spirit are antagonists, and body wins. The truth that lies in the ideal – Jude's vain aspirations to a life in the ivory towers of Christminster, the beauties of the New Testament, the life of the mind – is destroyed by the attractiveness of Arabella's large breasts and her artificial dimple.

The mind–body tensions are also explicit, part of the shaping force of the novel itself. Jude's story, as he succumbs to Arabella's seduction or is rejected by Christminster because of his class, in effect dramatizes the death of the Enlightenment dream of disinterested knowledge. For Jude and Sue, all thought, all work, is conditioned by the material context of personal history; it is inevitably interested. So, at one point, when the community is harassing Sue and Jude from their ecclesiastical work because they are not married, Sue exclaims, "I wish we could both follow an occupation in which personal circumstances don't count." Jude's response is almost an allegory of Hardy's relation to fiction and poetry: "I am not skilled in those ... I ought to take to bread-baking ... But even a baker must be conventional to get customers" (Bk 5, ch. 6, p. 376).

The aesthetic power of the book inheres partly in the constant playing out of this tension between two externalized aspects of the self, the mind and the body, or convention and rebellion. Sue's right-minded openness and hostility to convention are undercut by a visceral incapacity to live out her ideas. In the fates of Sue and Jude, Hardy moves through his at least quasi-materialism to the brink of a radical questioning of the whole set of assumptions that connects virtue with truth, truth with virtue, and he undercuts established ideas of character, meaning, order, and stability. The incompatibility between mind and matter produces a Nietzschean sense that all ideas of order are fictions imposed by the phenomenon of human consciousness on a matter entirely indifferent to it. But Hardy never treats this development with Nietzschean, or, one might say, Lawrentian exuberance. It is always a loss. A world in which mind and body are incompatible but yoked is deeply uncomfortable, one in which the realist's truth, through which worldly difficulties might be overcome, looks more like fiction than science. Pursuing truth in the manner of the *Bildungsroman* – of which *Jude* is a self-consciously negative example – can only lead to pain and loss. Many have called the book an "inverted Bildungsroman."[13]

The way out that Hardy explored was in aesthetic sacrifice of the self, dramatized in the stance of his strangely remote narrator who is protected from pain by his distance from the event. This "sacrifice" is importantly different from Sue's, whose ultimate humiliation of the flesh is required because she has allowed herself to be "touched" in the first place; that is, she has engaged with feeling, fallen in love, had desires at all. The narrator's detachment can get him only a short way. His narratives demonstrate that it is impossible for the characters to protect the spirit from the body, from the pulls of desire and the contingencies of the material world. But the artist himself survives not by working toward the redemptive powers of literal truth, but by turning from the task of an accurate representation of an increasingly elusive material reality, to the formally and aesthetically satisfying presentation of a virtually allegoric world too painful and too unstable to inhabit. It is a world and a novel, as he put it in his preface to the first edition, describing "a deadly war between flesh and spirit" (p. 39).

Seen abstractly, as *Jude* tends too often to do, it becomes too programmatic for the brilliantly imagined world that Jude and Sue inhabit. In *The Well-Beloved*, Hardy gives up on the primacy of the realist enterprise and plays out the question of the pursuit of the ideal in a form that is more suited to fairy tale repetition than to naturalism. *The Well-Beloved* completes and plays variations on *Jude the Obscure.*

Novels themselves, as Hardy's insistent antinaturalism implied, are forced into self-division: aspiring to truthfulness, they cannot be taken as representations of the real world but are rather ideal constructions imposed upon a material reality that is without ideals or ideas. At one point in his notes, Hardy underlines a key phrase from a discussion of Lange's *The History of Materialism and the Criticism of Its Present Importance* (1879): "all happiness lies in self-deception." He emphasizes that "fancies" that in no way answer to things in themselves "can afford him a felicity which nothing can replace."[14] In effect, as John Kucich suggests, in the late novels, the virtue of truth is displaced by a commitment to the aesthetic.[15] The material world, so unideal, is enmeshed in the ideal, which it generates. Following Von Hartmann and Schopenhauer, among others, Hardy gives up on the power of rationality to represent the material world and finds that consciousness and feeling are simply incompatible with their progenitor. Material parent and ideal child have no family resemblances.

Hardy never explicitly argued that his fictions affirmed their own unreality; at their least "real" they are "seemings." As ever committed to "truth," he claimed that it could only represent reality by distorting it. In one of his best-known comments on art, he wrote:

> Art is a changing of the actual proportions and order of things so as to bring out more forcibly than might otherwise be done that feature in them which appeals most strongly to the idiosyncrasy of the artist ... Art is a disproportioning – (i.e., distorting, throwing out of proportion) – of realities, to show more clearly the features that matter in those realities, which, if merely copied or reported inventorially, might possibly be observed, but would more probably be overlooked. (*LW*, p. 239)

The curious contradictions and the formal symmetry of *Jude* evolved from this mixture of epistemology, aestheticism, morality, and defensiveness. Hardy had not quite given up on material reality. We have seen that over and over again, in other novels at least, he found a way to re-enchant it. At the same time, he was convinced that science was giving him a pretty accurate reading of it. But art defies the conditions science was reporting.

Hardy's artful good look at the worst partly belies his insight into the way the body's interference makes knowing the truth an ultimate impossibility. As Hillis Miller long ago argued, and as I have emphasized in earlier chapters, the Hardyan narrator aspires to that condition of disembodied release from desire that he will not allow to his characters – Elizabeth-Jane's thoughts at the end of the *Mayor* come close to achieving that. In *Jude*, the defensiveness and awkwardness are clear as the narrator announces at the start of one chapter, "The purpose of a chronicler of moods and deeds does not require him to express his personal views upon the grave controversy above given" (Bk 5, ch. 5, p. 357). In *Jude*, Hardy's normally austere narrator is even more self-effacing than usual.

He refers to himself as "the chronicler of these lives" (Bk 6, ch. 10, p. 484), and he refrains from those extraordinary and enchanted descriptions of the natural world that sometimes overwhelm the narrative and to which I will return in the last chapter. *Jude* moves predominantly through dialogue, and the narration carries with it the authority of a detached observer's registration of what people say and do. Thus, while Jude's story enacts the discontinuity between the inextricably bound body and mind, and the unreliability of mind, the narrator's voice establishes a clear vision of *that* truth. Even when he becomes gnomic and aphoristic, there is something about the style that makes it feel like precise description of the way things are. Describing Jude as a very young man lost in his studies of Latin, and needing help from someone, the narrator straightforwardly asserts, "But nobody did come." That sequence became famous because Hardy powerfully adds, "because nobody does" (Bk 1, ch. 4, p. 22). It looks like a simple description, but obviously is not that at all. The artist becomes once again a figure of epistemological and moral eminence, dispelling the fantasies of order and the enchantments imposed on reality by desire disguised as consciousness; but he replaces them with his own fantasies of an order perhaps more rigorous than that he dispels. The vision is possible only by disembodying the visionary, by dying to desire.

At the start of his "Science of Fiction," Hardy applauds the "exercise of the Daedalian faculty for selection and cunning manipulation" (*PW*, p. 134). This brief essay implies the accessibility of truth "to science" but at the same time argues that attempting to reproduce "in its entirety the phantasmagoria of experience with infinite and atomic truth, without shadow, relevancy or subordination" is impossible, and, implicitly, not to the point of art. "Nothing but the illusion of truth can permanently please . . . a more natural magic has to be supplied" (p. 135). By the end of his novel-writing career Hardy clearly preferred fictions that revivify by making real order out of the felt randomness of the material world and, through human feeling, imposing a value in which it is a strain to believe but about which one continues to care.

Hardy, who read and admired Pater, with his new aesthetic registration of the hard, solipsistic, and materialistic implications of science,[16] almost certainly absorbed from Pater some of that preoccupation with individual perspective, some of that destabilizing of representational "truth," and its severance from the beautiful. He moves toward the sort of ironic position articulated wittily by Oscar Wilde in "The Critic as Artist," itself indebted to Darwin's way of representing the world.[17] Hardy, of course, does not play the paradoxes latent in this way of seeing into humor, as Wilde did, but the kinship is clear. The quest for scientific truth does not lead to intellectual and spiritual redemption; it is likely to lead to death, either for the knower or for the being known. The pursuit of truth for its own sake depends on a prior faith, faith in the ultimate moral value of truth. Kucich argues that Hardy affirms "aesthetic consciousness as the single area in which honesty can survive – and then only by candidly denying, within art, the moral possibility of truth" (p. 201). Value inheres in the ideal, in art itself, in making the world, not simply representing it. This makes the tragic story of *Jude*, and it makes the embittered first version and the deeply disenchanted second version of *The Well-Beloved* (1897).

CHAPTER 4

From Mindless Matter to the Art of the Mind
The Well-Beloved

The Well-Beloved is *Jude* revisited, more playfully, more overtly concerned with art, more overtly preoccupied with the relation between the ideal and the real. Its "fantastic" qualities reflect a yet more overt preoccupation with art than *Jude*'s more gritty realism allowed. Again, it is concerned with art in contention with a world from which the natural theological imagination of artistic design and construction has been withdrawn. There is nobody out there but nature itself designing things. The only designer is the human artist, much of whose creation is the imposition of form or design on the undesigned and largely happenstance world. Odd though the novel may seem, then, it is not an aberration in Hardy's fictional oeuvre, but an almost logical conclusion to his career as a novelist.

We might note the recurrence of a familiar Hardyan motif – the return(s) of the native. In his 1912 preface, Hardy calls his protagonist "a native of natives," a child of the isolated ancient peninsula that is the locus of the action, who returns with the skills of a modern artist to the source of both his life and his art. A different kind of Clym Yeobright, a different kind of Grace Melbury. Looking at *The Well-Beloved* as continuous with earlier Hardy will help suggest a development in which he increasingly fore-grounds art itself not only as a central concern of most of his novels, but as the most valuable instrument to resist the disasters he regularly dramatizes.

At first glance, *Jude the Obscure* and *The Well-Beloved* would seem creations of two different writers: *Jude*, naturalistically concerned to emphasize and expose social injustice and to come to terms with the way the claims of the body override any less material power – a combination that is traced in the tragic decline of the protagonist; *The Well-Beloved*, obsessed with the status of the ideal, with the temperament of the artist and with the relation of art to personal behavior. Hardy himself, in his Preface to *The Well-Beloved*, notes that it differs "from all or most others of the series in that the interest aimed at is of an ideal or subjective nature, and frankly fantastic, verisimilitude in the sequence of events has been sub-ordinated to the said aim" (*WB*, p. 4).

The difference, note, is in the "subjectivity," but it is certainly not in the novel's themes, not even in many of its plot elements and characterizations. Jocelyn Pierston and Jude Fawley are both questers after the ideal, Pierston, the artist, ever seeking the "well-beloved" in earthly incarnation, Jude seeking in the distant lights of Christminster the scholarly life. For both, the actual embodiments of those ideals are the problems; the material can contain the ideal for only a moment, and the consequence of the instability and inaccessibility of the ideal is disaster, though in very different modes in the different novels: *The Well-Beloved* is "fantastic." Yet both books are meticulously structured so that the triumph of the material is artfully embodied in a literary form that, like its protagonists, aspires to the ideal and the beautiful.[1]

The focal figure is an artist, not a working man, wealthy rather than poor. He works in the adamant stone that Jude must work in as well, and he embodies in that stone the ideal that he cannot sustain in life. By way of such embodiment, he becomes a great success, but can only continue to be successful as long as he believes in the "well-beloved." If the plotting of Jocelyn Pierston's life challenges verisimilitude, the book remains convinc-ingly representational in its framing context, and its formally symmetric structure reflects patterns regularly recurring in Hardy's other fictions – *The Mayor of Casterbridge* and *Jude*, most obviously. While it is, particu-larly at the start, almost whimsically or farcically comic, it moves toward an embittered end from which the ideal is also banished. The kind of preoccupation, which in *Tess* is explored through Angel Clare's rejection of the material Tess whom he had idealized, in *The Well-Beloved* occurs on almost every page pushing up from subtext and requiring all but explicit discussion of sex, particularly premarital sex. It is worth adding, moreover, that only the strange fantastic plotting keeps it from seeming even more intensely anti-marriage and more hostile to vulgarizing modernity than *Jude*. It is quite explicit about the ugliness of modern architecture, of commercial competition, and of the new suburbia, and it registers the difficult modern trade-off between the utilitarian and the traditional and beautiful.

Both books might be recognized as quest narratives. If *Jude* works out the Quixote motif in the life of a lower-class figure, *The Well-Beloved* works it out in the life of an artist. Jude is overcome in his ideal yearnings by the obduracy of his own materiality as much as by the social conventions that constrict him; sexuality and susceptibility to alcohol give a central physical basis to the failure of his Quixotic pursuit of the ideal in Christminster. Pierston is defeated in his yearnings by the sheer otherness and material reality of many women. He finds his ideal, at 20-year intervals, with each Avice when she is very young (the interval between the first and the second is occupied with his idealizing but distinctly material relationship with Marcia Bencomb). For both Jude and Jocelyn, the inextricable binding of the ideal with the material makes for failure, but Pierston understands from the start what Jude doesn't really learn, that the "ideal" woman is ideal only for a fleeting moment. The material embodiment might change at any time; the artist remains constant in his love of the ideal. Although he is conventional enough, like Jude, to be willing to marry the "well-beloved" when he finds it materialized, momentarily, in a woman, the first chapter makes clear that the well-beloved is always on the move, can take any bodily shape, and will not linger for long in any one. Pierston the protagonist is, in this respect, almost the reverse of Jude. A pig's pizzle makes Jude marry Arabella. In the first few chapters, Pierston commits to marry and doesn't marry two women, while finding in many others who flit through his experience embodiers of the ideal – he is a philandering idealist on a quest for an ever-moving ideal of the beautiful.

Art is the expression of consciousness, which Hardy saw as an almost inexplicable add-on to the evolution of the material world (essential to Darwin's great achievement was his power to explain the evolution of organisms without drawing on conscious design at all). It is the cosmic aberration, "consciousness," that allows the imagination of constancy, and thus the constancy that Pierston feels for his ideal. It is also, as we have seen in other Hardy novels, a source of great pain. It is what marks humans as distinct and what dooms them to lives of disappointment and loss. The artist is its fullest embodiment.

The Well-Beloved locks us so thoroughly inside Jocelyn Pierston's temperament that, like *Jude*, it almost ignores the natural vibrant physical world that, as I have been arguing throughout this book, provides a vital counterpoint to the protagonists' dark stories and may be – in its registration – the very apex of Hardy's achievement as artist. *Jude*'s austerity in providing that counterpoint is mirrored in *The Well-Beloved*, although the latter novel regularly reminds the reader, often in extraordinarily rich descriptive passages, of the rocklike materiality of the world to which Pierston returns, and from which he draws the raw material of his sculptures. The novel both escapes the material reality that Lawrence so admired in Hardy's work and, at the same time, knowingly leaves its protagonists there after the well-beloved escapes. Hardy's full turn to art might be thought of as allegorized in Pierston's quest. Hardy both knows that the ideal has no place in the material world, and works as novelist to create the ideal that, as living entangled being, neither he nor Pierston can sustain.

The Well-Beloved confirms how crucial the counterpoint with the represented vitality of the nonhuman world is to Hardy's fiction. It does that first, in its beautiful insistence on the place, the Isle of Slingers, alternately connected to and cut off from the rest of England by a narrow strip of stony land, and second, by its repeated refusal of the ideal nature of the women in whom Pierston alternately finds the idea. The stone is alive; the women are alive and like the stones are independent of Pierston's consciousness, but, unlike the stone, they are not malleable.

But Hardy is experimenting here, reinventing his fiction so as to explore the hidden side of the material realities in which his fictions so excelled. The idealism of Angel Clare or of Henry Knight becomes the absolute center of the narrative. Interestingly here, the idealism does not lead to the terrible destructiveness that follows when the ideal encounters the reality of an individual human being like Elfride or Tess. Such encounters form the core of the drama in the earlier books. The possibility of that destructiveness remains, but the focus here is on art, which is the fullest expression of human consciousness and can be creative and beautiful. Life, in the mindless indifference of material processes, is cruelly indifferent, but the mind that misreads Tess is aware of nature's indifference and feels the cruelty of that indifference.

Here again, as always at the basis of Hardy's art, is a continuing preoccupation with how one knows, with the miracle and aberration of intelligence, and with the way our power of knowing enables art and obliges us to feel for other living beings. The crisis of *The Well-Beloved* has to do with the question of whether it is possible to sustain the ideal, through art, and thus to be able to render with almost tactile richness, the beauty and complexity of the material world, and at the same time to avoid the disasters, tragic for Elfride and Tess, that aspiration to the ideal seems to inflict in this absolutely material world.

I

In a recent essay on Hardy, Hillis Miller claims that Hardy shares the modernist emphasis on "the isolation and incommunicability of individual human experience," on the dissolution of community, on religious skepticism, and on tragic outcomes.[2] But Miller does not mention what Suzy Anger has emphasized, Hardy's preoccupation with the powers, limits, and deceptions of consciousness, or Hardy's persistent concern with the nature of consciousness itself as it finds itself locked in the material conditions of the body.[3] Understanding more about this preoccupation might help in understanding why, as Miller puts it, Hardy does not *seem* to share with modernists an "increased complexity in narratological devices" and "self-conscious reflection on what literature is and what it can do" (p. 433). Hardy's artfulness is of a different kind, but no less concerned with both consciousness and art. It is not surprising that Miller omits this aspect of Hardy's work because, in his earlier study, one of the finest critical readings of Hardy that we have, Miller claims that Hardy "does not turn from what he sees to investigate the realm of interior space."[4]

It is easy to assume that exploration of that interior space requires the "inward turn," and entails throwing the action inside. The forms of a novel's language, the shape of the narrator's consciousness and of the implicit consciousness of the author, would, in modernist literature, become themselves the story's subject as form and content blend into each other. The movements of the characters' minds become more important than the "story" – in effect they *are* the story. So while James has been honored by representation in classes on modern or modernist fiction, Hardy, born only three years before him, turns up only in classes in Victorian fiction. Poor Hardy, it seemed, is thus left among the Victorians, insisting on telling stories, quite extravagant ones, and describing *things*, not minds.

But to come adequately to terms with Hardy's art, it is important to attend to the way he actually does emphasize, beyond the objectively described world, the consciousness of the observer describing it. In Miller's early, classic study, he argued that all of Hardy's narrations are "objective," representing the external world without exploration of the mind perceiving. This perception seems to me both crucially important and yet only partially right. Hardy's narrations do not so much explore consciousness as represent it in action, in contest with itself, in hiding from the consequences of its perceptions. They imply a distinctly Darwinian idea: consciousness itself might be thought of as a thing, a product of natural processes, like rocks and trees. For Hardy, no internal exploration of consciousness, such as was to be favored in modernist narrative, could satisfactorily clarify the mind's working. Consciousness itself, driven by forces it does not understand, both makes the world and separates humans from it.

An idiosyncratic equivalent of modernist narrative complexity and self-consciousness about art is woven deep into Hardy's prose, as he considers the role of consciousness in a world with which it is incompatible. For Victorian naturalists, all phenomena were to be understood as explicable in terms of laws now in operation, and this was increasingly accepted as just as true for humans as it was for stars. "The final problem," John Tyndall argued in his essay "Science and Man," "is this. Are the brain, and the moral and intellectual processes known to be associated with the brain – and as far as our experience goes indissolubly associated – subject to the laws which we find paramount in physical nature?"[5] In this respect, the nonmaterial consciousness and "spirit," insofar as the scientific naturalists allowed the word, were mysteries that they could not fit into their science, and that they wanted *not* to need for the explanation of any natural phenomenon, including human activity. Remember the telling title of one of T. H. Huxley's most famous essays, "On the Hypothesis That Animals Are Automata, and Its History."

Consider also the sentence preceding Darwin's famous single allusion to humans in *On the Origin of Species*, "Light will be thrown on the origin of man and his history": "Psychology," he says, "will be based on a new foundation, that of the necessary acquirement of each mental power and capacity by gradation" (*OS*, p. 488). His point is that the mind is not a gift of some designing spiritual power (as even A. R. Wallace, the co-discoverer of natural selection, was to come to believe) but has been developed through the mindless material and stochastic processes of natural selection; there is nothing casual about Darwin's decision, in sneaking in a quick allusion to the implications for humanity of his theory, that the first area of knowledge he points to as affected by this materialist interpretation will be "psychology." The most stunning aspect of his theory, and one that has been picked up again with a vengeance in our own time, is that, as much as the adaptive feathering of a bird or the long neck of a giraffe, the way people think and behave is determined by natural selection. As the rapid expansion of physiological psychology in Hardy's time makes evident, Victorian science responded to Darwin's suggestion, and its literature was an important part of Hardy's own reading. In one of his literary notebooks, Hardy copies some lines of G. H. Lewes:

> Physiology begins to disclose that all the mental processes were (mathematically speaking) functions of physical processes, i.e. – varying with the variations of bodily states; & this was declared enough to banish for ever the conception of a Soul, except as a term expressing certain functions.[6]

The irony is then that the discoveries that banish the soul intensify concern with the operations of mind. As narrator after narrator of Hardy's novels registers with loving or appalled particularity the details and the texture of the natural world, he invariably tells stories about the contrasting way in which characters actually perceive it. While readers cannot fail to be aware of the tensions and the differences, it might not be so obvious that in exploring and dramatizing these disparities, Hardy is also, and primarily, testing out the ironic oddities of consciousness itself.

Problems of this kind multiplied in the writing of scientists and thinkers whom Hardy knew and, for the most part, admired. If the physical laws scientists believed in were in operation, and thus matter can only be moved by matter, how can mind move muscles or affect our nerves? If all things, including humanity and its multifarious forms of behavior, are subject to the laws governing matter and are to be explained naturalistically, how did consciousness, which seems unembodied, get in there? Is there any reason it should be there? Of what use are the pain, anxiety, memory, and aspiration that mind makes possible? If the world mindlessly observes natural law, are there any intrinsic values in nature? If not, is mind, a nonmaterial aberration in a materialist world, fundamentally incompatible with the mindless and valueless world in which it moves? Is it possible that a nonmaterial "secretion of the brain" is capable of describing accurately "the natural system"? And perhaps the first issue that almost everyone concerned with this physiological understanding of consciousness had to address is what happens to the idea that humans have free will, and are therefore responsible for their choices? What happens to the idea of freedom and the notion of a distinctive "self" apart from the accidents of the flesh?

At one point in his notebooks, Hardy talks directly about this problem, invoking a hypothesis that represents mind as never interfering in the course of physical events, but "at best representing a mere inner aspect of the outward frame of things – a sort of backwater from the stream of physical forces" (I, p. 128). This may seem merely abstract epistemology, but consider Tess's story and the question of her virtue and innocence and one can see how these problems are assimilated into the very texture of Hardy's prose.

But post-Darwinian science not only challenged the ideas of the self and ethics. Both Lamarck and Darwin tried to demonstrate that scientific language did *not* describe nature as it was, but imposed upon it an order and significance that might have made it accessible to human study and perhaps manipulation, but that misrepresented it in so doing. "What is the whole physical life," Walter Pater famously asked, "but a combination of elements to which science gives their names?"[7] The connection between

Hardy's preoccupation with art, perhaps even as a saving force, and Pater's work, to which I have pointed in the "Interlude," is clear enough in Pater's very post-Darwinian "Conclusion" to *The Renaissance*, an essay that scandalized many and that Pater temporarily withdrew from his famous book. Art, like scientific language, registers not the reality of matter out there, but the activity of the mind in here. "The poetry of a scene," Hardy wrote, "varies with the minds of the perceivers. Indeed, it does not lie in the scene at all" (*LN*, I, p. 52). This shift of perspective is consonant with later aesthetic theorizing about art.[8] Oscar Wilde's paradoxical talks of art as a form of lying, creative rather than merely descriptive, is akin to Hardy's argument that "Art is a disproportioning – (i.e., distorting, throwing out of proportion) – of realities." To be more true than the truth, as Hardy sought to be, means, in Wilde's terms, "lying."[9]

The sense that the world begins not with the fiat of an intelligent being but with the clumsy, unintelligent hit and miss movements of nature, written deep into Hardy's bones and prose, reveals itself particularly in reversals and paradox. This fundamental perception of an apparently intelligently designed world created by unintelligent algorithms was a key to Darwin's way of seeing, and it reverses common sense. Order, value, and meaning, previously assumed to be intrinsic to the very nature of created things, disappear from this mindless world, and reenter only through the activities of human consciousness, indispensable while it is itself the product of mindlessness. We have no access to the matter we purport to describe, but are locked into our own sensory equipment. The world only *seems* to come to our attention as objective reality, already ordered, meaningful, thick with value. And so Hardy's narrations, as Miller has so well described them, consistently appear to be "objective." But the conclusion must be that it is the human mind, not nature itself, that creates the ostensibly objective order and value and that makes our lives worth living. That image that Hardy drew, of his spectacles laid before a drawn rural scene upon which they look, comes increasingly to mind. The novel as a series of seemings is not far from Pater's famous formulation: what we describe is not "the object as in itself it really is," but "one's own impression as it really is" (*Renaissance*, p. x).

"Oh you materialist," Darwin slyly reprimanded himself in one of his Mutation notebooks in 1838. "Why," he asks, "is thought being a secretion of the brain more wonderful than gravity a property of matter? It is our arrogance, it is our admiration of ourselves."[10] Materialist Darwin was, as were most of the scientific naturalists who spread his word through the culture, despite their rejection of the term in its full metaphysical significance; Darwin only allowed it in his notebooks. As Phillip Mallett puts it, the idea that "underlies most of Hardy's work" is that "human consciousness is the unintended byproduct of accidental organizations of matter" (*CTH*, p. 26).

The downgrading of mind from soul and divine gift to the accidental product of mere matter ironically makes it more interesting and more problematic for modernist writers – and for Hardy. Certainly, it made it more interesting and worrisome for Darwin himself. Near the end of his life, he wrote to William Graham, "The horrid doubt always rises whether the convictions of man's mind, which has been developed from the mind of the lower animals, are of any value or at all trustworthy."[11] With this question, Darwinian materialism and denial of intentional energy in the workings of nature tended not to diminish but to intensify artists' and scientists' quests for patterns of order and meaning, and thus to force them to encounter directly the newly problematic world of consciousness. The "objectivity" of narration that Miller rightly notes in Hardy's fiction is ultimately secondary to the subjectivity that underlies it. Summarizing some ideas of Comte, Hardy writes in his notes:

> Excess of Subjectivity during the nonage of individuals or race – then Objective method arose – increased: Subjectivity has less share in framing our theories: but, continuing in this course, the modern *ascendency of Objectivity* by repressing the imagination under pretext of reality, tends to *idiocy*. But *Subjectivity in a regenerated form*, exercised on the future from materials of the past, will ultimately rule. (*LN*, I, p. 76)

If human consciousness, not a divine fiat, created the meaning of the world, "consciousness" becomes important not only out of scientific curiosity but because, for better or worse, it is the one thing that distinguishes humans from the rest of the material world. As Wilde was to imply, it is the lying source of the ideal, of art, and of creativity. If there is intention in nature, humans put it there. Where Wilde saw its comic implications, Hardy saw the incompatibility of mind with nature as a source of tragedy; consciousness was a dangerous and fascinating and extraordinarily generative anomaly in a world of matter. It is the source of art, and it guarantees its human value.

Hardy's obsession with the way the mind works is not like that, for example, of George Eliot because he had in his bones and as the most solid foundation of his art a deep feeling for the physicality of the world, a feeling that made him so fascinating to Lawrence. His art is, as it were, the art of uncanny adeptness at making his way in the woods, of understanding the traces that nature inevitably leaves, of reading the meaning of a world without meaning. I would suspect, however, that Lawrence felt that there was too much mind in Hardy's art, that he was too much a part of a culture that was everywhere turning the action inside, even as his finest writing is about the outside. While he was certainly not a "psychological novelist," his fame as a writer emphasizing the powerlessness of mind against the forces and materials of nature tends to distract interest from his continuing preoccupation with mind, or with "temperament," as in the subtitle of *The Well-Beloved*. Hardy creates plots about and is clearly fascinated by the mind's powers, its deceptions (self-deceptions), its susceptibility to pain, but also and emphatically by the time of *The Well-Beloved*, by its creativity. It is not, after all, a trivial matter that part of the plot of *The Woodlanders* revolves around Fitzpiers' desire (however superficial it turns out to be) to study Grammer Oliver's brain – the material casing that houses and thus determines consciousness. The mind is seated in the raw material of the brain, and yet it determines all the negotiations of his characters not only with the mindless natural world but also with other consciousnesses. Through the voice of his narrators, Hardy demonstrates how their consciousness and the consciousness of his characters do not so much register the objective reality of the world as create it. What we perceive turns the tangled bank of reality into the ordered, the beautiful, the ideal, or even the shapely reverse of the ideal. The chancy, mixed, and mindless ways of the material world are the ever-looming and always immensely important context for his narratives. Art is, in this respect, the fullest expression of mind, and Hardy's materialism verges on idealism, although in the end the idea and ideal will always succumb to the relentless insistence of the material. So here I am shifting the emphasis of Miller's analysis and taking up another suggestion of Suzy Anger: "Consciousness," she claims, "might be said to be Hardy's central concern in his writing, from *Desperate Remedies* through *The Dynasts*" (Anger, p. 495).

Hardy's characters tend not to be reflective before they act but can become introspective after their actions, trying to understand their own behavior, which might well seem inconsistent with their desire. But for the most part, consciousness is expressed beyond thinking, reflection, and introspection, and cannot quite keep up with itself. It is this insight that leads to Lawrence's favorable readings of Hardy. So *The Mayor of Casterbridge* is built on the whim of Henchard's determination to sell his wife, but in un-Lawrentian ways he turns against his own instincts in his longing for respectability, which leads him virtually always to repent his actions. Or, within a few pages of *A Pair of Blue Eyes*, Elfride plans to run away with Stephen, changes her mind, changes her mind again, and, after finally eloping to London, asks to return even before she gets there. Kay Young traces this kind of behavior throughout Hardy's fiction, particularly in Sue Bridehead's jumping out the window twice in *Jude the Obscure*.[12] There is no Jamesian analysis of the movements of Sue's mind, but as W. K. Clifford had argued in a famous essay, you do "nothing else from morning to night but *change your mind*."[13] We do so not with mindful attention to alternatives, but driven by material and often preconscious urgencies. Even in the mind the body triumphs.

As Anger shows, the physiological reading of mind manifests itself in the way Hardy imagines character and develops those characteristically elaborate and overplotted narratives. "You see," he writes to a friend, "that the assumption that intelligent beings arise from the combined action of unintelligent forces is sufficiently probable for imaginative writing."[14] At his best as a writer when the clumsy philosophizing and polysyllabic Latinate diction give way to a beautiful precision, he registers apparently objective perceptions, and traces, usually without analysis, their rapid changes, giving the impression of a singular way of seeing. That way, beyond the limitations of conventional ways of imagining character, he gives to his narratives a texture of verisimilar irrationality. Characters are not, finally, driven by mind, but by surges of feeling, by instinct, by sexual impulses. Their failures are partly the result of the constraints that Lawrence despised – surges of what might be thought of as irrational rationality that denies and constrains natural human energies. The fear of loss of respectability, the conventions of ordinary social ordering, is both his characters' limitation and Hardy's own.

The novels persistently dramatize the disparity between event and reflection; they are "objective," in Miller's sense, at the same time as they dramatize the difference between the way characters imagine each other and the way they really are, and between intentional and what we might call instinctual behavior. Kay Young, building on Miller's earlier work, writes that Hardy does not pause to analyze consciousness or motives, but narrates extraordinary leaps of consciousness: for the most part, "a Hardy character exists in a mental landscape of 'unthinking consciousness' or 'after-thought consciousness'" (p. 139). These disparities, so ingeniously demonstrated by Miller, play out in a broad variety of ways a familiar underlying and often overt concern of novel after novel – the epistemological and ethical disconnection between mind and matter. The characters ever too little know themselves, but create with their unthinking consciousness the world they inhabit, as the narrator finds patterns and meaning in the juxtaposition of those minds. The anomaly, the incompatibility of mind with the matter that produced it, helps explain why Hardy insisted so frequently that art was a seeming, a shaping, a design, the warp and woof of a beautiful tapestry. I quote here a famous entry from his notebooks, where he makes this point:

> As in looking at a carpet, by following one colour a certain pattern is suggested, by following another colour, another; so in life the seer should watch that pattern among general things which his idiosyncrasy moves him to observe, and describe that alone. This is, quite accurately, a going to Nature; yet the result is no mere photography, but purely the product of the writer's own mind. (*LWTH*, p. 158)

The Well-Beloved might then be seen as Hardy's fantasy on this theme, a fantasy that brings him close to the modernism his objective, "Victorian" style would suggest he never reached. The novel juxtaposes Pierston's art with nature. It does not so much explore Pierston's mind in the mode of modernism, as it makes that mind the filter of nature for the sake of art. Late nineteenth-century preoccupation with the psychology of characters exploited the failures of mind to comprehend nature's mindless forces or the realities of other consciousnesses. The mind, no longer a divine gift but a blundering alien in nature, encountered problems in every phase of its activities. No writer more than Hardy so thrives in his fictions on mis-understanding. No writer succeeds more powerfully in turning those misunderstandings into art.

Pierston instinctively turns real bodies into ideals, into art. Such acts in Hardy, even if in narrative they seem a bit crazy, allow some kind of reconciliation with the not quite knowable substance of the real world. This unknowable reality intimates its driving and vital presence in the images, usually of natural phenomena, that Hardy builds richly into almost all but his last two novels. But there too in other ways, partly by suggesting how the triumph of the merely material world crushes possibility and the ideal, they suggest a Lawrentian understory of energy and vitality against which the organized plotting of the protagonist's lives is played out. The consequences of mind's incompatibility with matter and body may be disastrous, but art can make disaster into tragedy by imposing order and meaning on what is merely chance and mindless energy. It is the reason to live; it is the source of the pain that makes us sometimes wish, like little Father Time, not to.

II

The Well-Beloved was written first for serial publication in 1892, and greatly revised as a whole in 1897, after Hardy had decided to move entirely from fiction to poetry. In it, Hardy sets consciousness in the context of a vast block of stone and yet makes consciousness everything, even while showing that it is rarely "rational," and a mere accident of natural laws. The novel's preoccupation with the idea is encased in very hard, adamant materiality. But the solid stone itself, surrounded by the ever-changing sea, is itself alive, while the community that inhabits it has roots in an ancient culture isolated – at least until the end of the novel – from the transformations of modernity. The stone, constantly drawn upon for commercial and artistic use, is alive and essential to all that follows. Returning to it, the native sees it as a stranger:

> The towering rock, the houses above houses, one man's doorstep rising behind his neighbor's chimney, the gardens hung up by one edge to the sky, the vegetables growing on almost vertical planes, the unity of the whole island as a solid and single block of limestone four miles long, were no longer familiar and commonplace ideas. All now stood dazzlingly unique and white against the tinted sea, and the sun flashed on infinitely stratified walls of oolite. (p. 9)

The poetic turn is suggested by the book's daring move beyond Hardy's usual precision of material description into a kind of agon between the material and the artist's fantastic imagination. The problem that lay behind Clym Yeobright's defeat, and the defeats and frustrations that, in various ways, had plagued a whole range of Hardy's protagonists, recur here in a less obviously tragic mode. The old mind–body problem is re-evoked as a problem of the relation of art to life. That consciousness and art belie reality in creating order and beauty becomes a running motif of the entire novel. Art seems to resist the mindless processes of natural law, but succumbs to mere matter when the artist gives up the quest for the ideal

The novel is prime evidence that Hardy was, like other modernists, intensely engaged with "self-conscious reflection on what literature" (or art) "is and what it can do." It plays extravagantly with any traditional realist notion of how novels might be organized – in its representation of the world and Pierston's consciousness as reflections of each other, in its increasingly incredible repetitions, in the way the literary and the ideal blend into and yet resist and comment on each other, and in its control of perspectives. The narrative may be "objective," but in effect it locks us into Pierston's mind, and although Hardy has no reputation for experimenting with free indirect discourse, a significant chunk of the novel reports Pierston's reflections in the third person form characteristic of that method. Because of its rigorous narrative control, as Hardy's narrator confines himself for the most part to the way Pierston perceives and understands his perceptions, it seems at times almost tongue-in-cheek about the reality of the ideal that drives him. It can hardly be an accident that the protagonist's name, Pierston, might well be heard as "pearce stone."

With very little of the building tension that characterizes the plots of Victorian novels, on the whole, *The Well-Beloved* is nevertheless heavily plotted, tracing with a kind of mad geometry Pierston's history in his pursuit of a "migratory, elusive idealization he called his Love," as that idealization "flits from human shell to human shell" (p. 13). Against the ideal that Pierston pursues, the novel focuses intensely on the deep materiality of the setting in which the ideal persists in showing herself. "The Isle of Slingers," that "solid and single block of limestone four miles long," is as important to the novel as any character, including Pierston himself. It is both dumb and valuable, valuable not intrinsically but in use, because it supplies stone to all of England and around the world. It is also literally the source of the story's materials and of Pierston's art. It is a mark of geological history with its "infinitely stratified walls of oolite," and in its transformation from the island it once was in geological time to the peninsula it has become, with its "long thin neck of pebbles 'cast up by the rages of the se' " (p. 9). This almost aggressively material stone slab is the place of birth, the place of death, the place from which the ideal emanates and into which it disappears, and the place to which the story constantly returns. Its sheer dumb materiality becomes part of the story's ideality as the material brain is the source of the mind's workings.

Although Pierston pursues an "indefinite number" of embodiments, the novel focuses on only four, all intimately enwound with the life and stone of the "Isle," and particularly, incredibly, on those three generations of Avices. Just as the Isle is the "shell" in which each character lives, each of these potential lovers for Pierston is a "human shell" in which, more or less briefly, Pierston's ideal settles. Pierston – like so many of Hardy's quasi-artist protagonists – feels himself cursed with an emotional youthfulness incompatible with his material aging. In a passage of free indirect discourse, Pierston is described as reflecting on this curse: "While his soul was what it was, why should he have been encumbered with that withering carcass without the ability to shift it off for another, as his ideal Beloved had so frequently done?" It is a realist's version of a myth whose very center is the split between mind and body. Like Tennyson's Tithonus, Pierston laments, "When was it to end – this curse of his heart not ageing while his frame moved naturally onward?" (p. 131). Pierston, "earth in earth," recognizes with his shriveling body the immortal beauty of the goddess, as he imagines her eternal return. But not as in Tennyson's "Tithonus," beyond the death he longs for. Death closes down conscious- ness and thus the ideal itself.

The madness of the book's geometry extends beyond the replication of loves, imagined as a single love. Pierston abandons the first Avice – interestingly because she does not want to indulge the ancient local tradition of having sex with her future husband just before the wedding. When she does not meet him, he switches his ever-moving ideal to another woman, Marcia. That then moves to the second Avice, who abandons him, for it turns out that she is already married. Not coincidentally, her husband is a worker in stone whose last name, like that of many of the islanders, is Pierston; a worker in stone, though not as artist, he is a mindless version of Pierston. Lover, beloved, and rival all become, at least nominally, versions of each other. Avice is married to one kind of stone worker, and sought by another, the sculptor. Again, in another Hardyesque coincidence that is not a coincidence, Pierston gives up the third Avice to the son of his first lover, Marcia. With familiar Hardyan irony, Pierston notes, "It is how I served her grandmother – One of Time's revenges" (p. 193). The almost claustrophobic symmetry makes the "realist" qualities of the book dreamlike, as though we are watching not the objective drama of a series of characters, but the movements of Pierston's mind.

Through it all, the fickle transience of Pierston's ideal reinforces the idea that mind has no intrinsic connection with body, although it requires embodiment. The strange plot helps explain why it is that Hardy was so unrelentingly unwilling to allow his aspiring protagonists the kind of fulfillment normally given to protagonists at the end of Victorian realist novels. Frustration in pursuit of the loved one marks the life of almost every protagonist of every Hardy novel, from *Far from the Madding Crowd* (although Oak finally does get to marry Bathsheba, it is largely because she can't bear the idea that he will go away and stop desiring her) to *The Woodlanders*, where Giles Winterborne dies just a few feet away from his untouchable beloved, Grace.

The Well-Beloved plays out the persistent Romantic notion that it is desire itself, not fulfillment, that gives meaning to life. It is desire, working on the mind's power to see, that gives the object, the shell, its meaning, and makes for the beautiful. Worse than the deep frustrations of the pursuit would be the actuality of consummation (which might also account, beyond his obvious personal experiences, for Hardy's consistently negative views of marriage, and Jude and Sue's reluctance to marry). Hardy's treatment of Pierston's longing for the ideal replays the Romantic conception of *la princesse lointain*. Pierston, for example, only recognizes Avice the first as the real embodiment of the ideal after he learns of her death. He can continue to regret her loss, or long for her replication and remain a successful artist, now that the possibility of consummation with her is safely gone. Pierston's art and the novel itself depend on this circular pattern. Only Pierston's loss of desire can bring his art and his novel to an end.

However interpreted, *The Well-Beloved* also suggests the incompatibility between the material world, including the body, and the sophisticated consciousnesses that somehow have emerged from it. It suggests that, as in Pierston's sculptures, the consciousness does not so much report the world as create it. Everything is created by the mind. Observing the second Avice from a distance out on the cliffs of the isle, Pierston reflects:

> How incomparable the immaterial dream dwarfed the grandest of substantial things, when here, between those three sublimities – the sky, the rock, and the ocean – the minute personality of this washer-girl filled his consciousness to its extremest boundary, and the stupendous inanimate scene shrank to a corner therein. (p. 102)

The creations of the mind – its perceptions saturated with desire – infuse with an "immaterial dream" the "minute personality," that is, the figure seen as tiny against the background of massive matter, "the sky, the rock, the ocean." It is the imagination of the artist, transforming the substance, but at the same time aware of the disparity between what the mind can see and the enormous inanimate reality that, by virtue of the creative power of desire, can seem to shrink matter into a corner.

But of course, the limestone block outside of Pierston's passionate perception remains dumbly unmoved. The role of the stone in the play of art and consciousness is emphasized particularly when the narrator notes that

> while the son had been modeling and chipping his ephemeral fancies into perennial shapes, the father had been persistently chiseling for half a century at the crude original matter of those shapes, the stern, isolated rock in the Channel; and by aide of his cranes and pulleys, his trolleys and his boats, had sent off his spoil to all parts of Great Britain. (p. 55)

The tension between the two kinds of sculpting marks the limits and tensions of the mind and of the artist at work. He and the stone worker use exactly the same materials. Whatever the realities of matter, Pierston, the sculptor, infuses it with beauty and feeling, carving and scraping away the dead stone; so Pierston the lover infuses the minute figure spied at a distance, the human body, the shell, with his ideal of the Well-Beloved. It is just this kind of projective activity, here seen as the lover-artist's pursuit of the ideal, that manifests itself, if less obviously, in Hardy's tragic stories.

The Well-Beloved is persistently self-conscious and implicitly uneasy about the creative (and deceiving) force of consciousness, and one of the marks of Hardy's thought and his art is that he does not forget the reality of that "objective" world of sky, rock, and ocean, which inevitably runs against the ideas – and desires – that impel the protagonists. Against the workings of consciousness, there is always in Hardy, and in *The Well-Beloved*, the forceful presence of material and mindless reality. It is the understory emerged now as thematically central. The human body, too, the "shell" into which the ideal beloved sometimes flits, is a material reality, if not mindless, and Hardy does not forget that either. In the great sweep of Hardy's fiction, the art and the material reality it must engage express each other forcefully, and Hardy struggles to invest the shell with life. The experiment of *The Well-Beloved* is somehow to find a way to recognize the life of the objects that are always perceived, always objects instead of subjects. Lawrence's interest in Hardy has to do with the way Hardy's prose renders with respectful attention the natural world's vitality and beauty, evoking the irrational, the mindless force that drives all life. So in the very first chapter, Pierston feels the warmth of the rock "in its afternoon sleep."

But the novel plays the game of reality/ideal primarily through questions of perception and perspective. Once again, the "shell" must be shown to pay the price for housing the ideal, even for a moment. *The Well-Beloved* plays less and more seriously with recognition of this price, which we have already seen paid by Tess, when the "shell," not her idealizer, suddenly becomes the subject, and the tables are turned on Pierston. We remember Angel telling Tess and turning her story into tragedy: "You were one person: now you are another." Pierston must feel the effect of himself being the embodied shell of an ideal. Or even further back, in *A Pair of Blue Eyes*, when Henry Knight learns that Elfride had been kissed before, she becomes a shell. There the almost absurdly excessive language points toward the virtually parodic quality of the extravagant plot of *The Well-Beloved*: "there had passed away a glory, and the dream was not as it was of yore."[15]

The realist novel and Hardy's art require distrust of the ideal even as they aspire to it. The bereft women are indeed bereft and tragic figures in their helpless and uncomprehending responses to rejection. But while Pierston does in effect deny the Avices' individual reality by thrusting his ideal on each, *The Well-Beloved* plays with point of view so that the tables are turned on the artist/dreamer. Even in this deliberate narrative inversion, *The Well-Beloved* enforces the realist lessons. Each Avice does much better than Tess or Elfride, when the ideal of the well-beloved slips from their bodies. In the end, it is Pierston, the perceiver, who becomes the perceived, who is embodied and abandoned by the narrative so that the novel is transformed from a Romantic quest comedy, to a realist narrative of disenchantment (more usually Hardy's mode). In the sequence about the second Avice (who, in her uneducated and lower-class person, is the apparent furthest from the ideal), there is a strikingly ironic moment when Pierston comes to recognize the human price of his idealizing artistic instinct. Avice explains to Pierston why, even if she were to be his young woman, it wouldn't have been for long:

> 'Tis because I get tired of my lovers as soon as I get to know them well. What I see in one young man for a while soon leaves him and goes into another yonder, and I follow, and then what I admire fades out of him and springs up somewhere else; and so I follow on, and never fix to one. (p. 103)

For Pierston, discovering that others also aspire to a Well-Beloved is shocking enough. But the hardest thing is to recognize that he is also a shell:

> This seeking of the Well-Beloved was, then, of the nature of the knife which could cut two ways. To be the seeker was one thing: to be one of the corpses from which the ideal had departed was another; and this was what he had become now, in the mockery of new days. (p. 104)

It is one of the characteristics of Hardy's art in any of its phases that his novels manifest an enormous sympathy for the individual, require attention to the pain of virtually all creatures, and certainly for the abandoned shells. Pierston both feels and enacts that double sense, the power and attraction of the ideal, the need and the pathos and the pain of the embodied individual. The novels are infused with this double sense, and much of their pathos and tragic force comes from the conflict between the workings of consciousness and desire and the realities of physical embodiment, which, reacting on the consciousness, produce a new kind of pain. In a way it is an old banality – romance does not last long beyond its first consummation. And yet in Hardy this disenchantment is accompanied by a sense that there is an enormous loss that comes with realism itself – the death of the desire that is based on an ever-receding ideal; it is the loss of enchantment. The mind creates its own reality, and that is more beautiful and more life-giving than life itself. The tragic excesses are, ironically, part of the work of imaginative projection: the mind creating an order in the symmetries that really do not exist in mindless nature. The tragedy might be seen to be as much the loss of the creative power of the mind as it is the real suffering that the imaginative artist Thomas Hardy describes as a consequence of that power.

But Hardy was probably too much the Victorian, too much the sensitive artist, and too aware of the pain involved in the normal processes of life as they are understood from his post-Darwinian perspective, to play the Wildean comic ironist to the hard realities of individual suffering. Much of the power of his art resides just in his ambivalence about the dualities of consciousness, the artist's gift that emerged mysteriously from raw matter. He does not, he could not, go all the way that Lawrence wanted, surrender to the overwhelming realities of the irrational world and celebrate them. In novel after novel, despite the grand-scale tragic blunders and disasters, despite the recognition of the massive indifference of the inanimate world to the strategies of consciousness, to human desires and dreams, Hardy implies a tenderness toward the merely and weakly human that emerges even in the relentless demonstration of each minute figure's smallness and irrelevance to the vast business of a cosmos driven by unintelligent forces – Huxley's "cosmic process." When Pierston finally returns to the Isle of Slingers, where he will have his last failed encounter with the Well-Beloved, he visits the second Avice, now ill and widowed. It is a moment of encounter with the individual reality of all those shells to whom, when his ideal escapes them, he has not been kind:

> Avice, who had been little in his mind of late years, began to renew for herself a distinct position therein. He was fully aware that since his earlier manhood a change had come over his regard of womankind. Once the individual had been nothing more to him than the temporary abiding-place of the typical or ideal; now his heart showed its bent to be a growing fidelity to the specimen, with all her pathetic flaws of detail; which flaws, so far from sending him further, increased his tenderness. This mature feeling, if finer and higher, was less convenient than the old.

Hardy's art at its best reveals that "growing fidelity to the specimen," to the individual rather than to one of the mind's fictions, that is, the species. Beyond all the philosophizing and all the cosmic lamentation, Hardy's art focuses on the price paid by the individual, not on some vague collective species called humanity. His constant insistence that he was not a philosopher and did not aim for philosophic consistency is manifest in this aspect of his novels, and in their ambivalence about this question of consciousness as creative and falsifying and consciousness as an aspect of materiality.

The hard reality of the merely physical ultimately determines almost everything. When the third Avice abandons Pierston for the son of his former lover, Pierston speaks to that lover, Marcia: "Don't regret it, Marcia. He shall not lose by it. I have no relation in the world except some twentieth cousins in this isle, of whom her father was one, and I'll take steps at once to make her a good match for him. As for me . . . I have lived a day too long" (p. 195). The duality of mind–body emerges again in the conflict between love of the specimen, and love of the ideal. At the moment of assuring that he will help the third Avice as he had helped the second, he also announces his wish for death. Pierston falls ill after the funeral of the second Avice, and, when he begins to recover, he discovers that his nurse through the worst of it has been Marcia. It is then that he realizes that he has been transformed, not like Tess by the perceptions of another, but by his own change of perspective, that is, his loss of the ideal, first, symbolically in the death of Avice; second, literally in the elopement of Avice; and third, "He was no longer the same man that he had hitherto been. The malignant fever, or his experiences, or both, had taken away something from him, and put something else in its place" (p. 197). Without the falsifying powers of consciousness that through unsatisfied desire create the ideal, there is nothing to keep the formerly youthful Pierston from the normal bodily processes of decay. Worn down in his status as "shell," as mere matter, as the aging Tithonus, by a lifetime of pursuit of the ideal, he cannot resume it. He has been defeated by his body at last. Without the pursuit of the ideal, he has lived a day too long.

The "artistic sense had left him," and it is replaced by the literal body. When he gets his body he loses his youthfulness – a metaphor, certainly, for artistic immortality. At no point, and certainly not in its ending, does the novel reconcile mind and body. But the last chapters are movingly devoted to a now desireless Pierston, shifting focus from the ideal and the false hopes of desire that make for art to the heavy, decaying presence of the body. It is almost a version of Dorian Gray, but without the evil. Marcia, for whom he forsook the first Avice, returns symmetrically in this phase of the novel, "An Old Tabernacle in a New Aspect," embarrassed by the physical decay hidden beneath her makeup:

the image and superscription of Age – an old woman, pale and shriveled, her forehead ploughed, her cheek hollow, her hair white as snow. To this the face he once kissed had been brought by the rasping, chiseling's, scourging, bakings, freezings of forty invidious years, by the thinklings of more than half a lifetime. (p. 200)

It is obviously not by chance that this description invokes metaphors of sculpture and stone work – nature itself, without the assistance of consciousness, carves out its images, is the ultimate sculptor, and the only consciousness is Marcia's own, whose "thinklings" are responsible for nature's sculpture.

The body unidealized returns and wreaks its vengeance, for, following the perverse logic of the book, Pierston, fastened to a dying animal, himself recovering from a serious ailment, marries her. The bodily ironies compound, for when Pierston marries Marcia, she is attacked by rheumatism, and "after being well wrapped up, was wheeled into the church in a chair." At the end, then, it is all body, and body in its natural state of decay, not Pierston's unnatural state of permanent adolescence.

The fulfillment of marriage, the happy ending of the Victorian novel, is in Hardy the end of desire and of art. In its last pages, the book invokes "Tithonus" directly: "Alas for this Grey Shadow, once a Man." In effect they are about the body's reemergence and dominance over the creative activity of the mind. "The artistic sense had left him, and he could no longer attach a definite sentiment to images of beauty recalled from the past. His appreciativeness was capable of exercising itself only on utilitarian matters" (p. 198). Rather, as Darwin describes himself near the end of his *Autobiography*, Pierston has lost the power of emotional responsiveness. He cannot read the material world and its stony matter into which he had previously poured his art, his feelings, and his imagination. The raw matter of the stone, which dominates the book, is important finally only for its utility, not for its potential to house the beautiful ideal. "Thank Heaven," Pierston says, "I am old at last."

The complexity of Hardy's attitude toward the creative power of mind and its power to shape reality gets a final twist as the book and Pierston run down. It might be suggested that the almost comic, self-consciously ironic *The Well-Beloved* is bleaker in implications than *Jude* itself. With the "extinction of the well-beloved," Pierston turns to local business and advances

a scheme for the closing of the old natural fountains in the Street of Wells, because of the possible contamination, and supplying the townlet with

water from pipes, a scheme that was carried out at his expense, as is well
known. He was also engaged in acquiring some moss-grown, mullioned
Elizabethan cottages for the purpose of pulling them down because they
were damp, which he afterwards did, and built new ones with hollow walls
and full of ventilators. (p. 205)

Hardy does not need at this point to emphasize the ambivalence. Pierston
has gone from being the artist to the practical man. He does good works at
the price of destroying the beauty and culture of his native place. He
marries a woman he doesn't love. He becomes a philanthropist.
The beautiful gives way to the merely moral, dealing practically with the
material world and letting the ideal go.

Hardy's preoccupation with respectability, dramatized so often in the
novels, also reemerges here in a way that suggests once again his great
discomfort with his own longing for it. The negative judgment of the
community, which seems able to catch any protagonist's slightest unconventional act, eventually usually compromises his protagonists. When Pierston
and Marcia resume their old friendship, they both are disturbed by the
neighbors' knowledge of their former romance, which leads to expectation
about appropriate behavior. Pierston complains: "It is extraordinary what an
interest our neighbours take in our affects . . . They say 'Those old folk ought
to marry; better late than never.' That's how people are – wanting to round
off other people's histories in the best machine-made conventional manner."
It is the story of Jude and Sue, in a less obviously tragic key.

Through all his life as an artist, and like his neighbors, Pierston has been
rounding off his subjects by imposing the ideal on a resistant materiality, yet
he complains here that the collective consciousness of the community wants
to impose its ideal on him. The difference is undoubtedly in the words
"convention" and "machine." Complain though he might, he gives in to
convention and decides to marry Marcia: "And so the zealous wishes of the
neighbours to give a geometrical shape to their story were fulfilled almost in
spite of the chief parties themselves" (p. 204). It is difficult not to recall here
how Hardy in novel after novel gives geometric shape to his stories – a maker
of the art that orders a wild nature. Here, Pierston makes clear that this is
a marriage of convention, not love: "I have no love to give you, you know,
Marcia . . . But such friendship as I am capable of is yours till the end"
(p. 204). And thus – a choice Hardy requires – the novel slips back from
romance to realism; Pierston slips from romantic artist to practical human.
The alternative, the continuing self-deception of a consciousness that imagines an ideal against the raw and unintelligent force of matter, is always
tragic – in the death of Henchard, or Winterborne, or Tess, or Jude.

As the book closes with the stone having lost its artistic potential for sculpture to become only an enormous utilitarian article for the improvement of society, and Pierston having become a shell from which the ideal has passed, it is tempting to invoke Wilde's praise of lying. The world is infused with meaning by the lies that people and artists use to impose order on it; the alternative is a morality and utility that forgo the imagination and beauty. Wilde treats with comedy and irony the same issues that Hardy explores in *The Well-Beloved*, and celebrates the deceptions of art. In face of a world that resists human desire, a world, as Wilde puts it, full of awful "black bugs," the mind creates the beautiful. It is all a lie, but the mindless processes of nature need the revision that human consciousness, susceptible to the pains it inevitably inflicts, can imagine for it. The order of art is the force that makes life worth living. But Hardy adds to this conception a recognition of the cost to the individual, the shell, of this false ordering and idealizing. The hard stone of the Isle of Slingers is put to creative use by human inventiveness. But the hard stone is subject to the processes of nature that recur through geological time and that transform human aspirations and ideals into minute figures in the process. The mind at once saves and compromises its possessors.

But there is yet a further irony here, beyond what the literal actions inside the text can intimate. All of these developments are the work of a novelist still self-consciously, if paradoxically, giving "geometric" shape through art to the ultimate triumph of the material – stone and human body – over the ideal. The novel gives shape to incompatible elements: Pierston's concern for the specimen, his loveless marriage to an early now decayed embodiment of the Well-Beloved, avoidance of the scene of Pierston's death, and a touchingly bathetic conclusion. The last word about Pierston is a critic's: he was "insufficiently recognized in his lifetime." All of this evokes a quite remarkable and touching sense of loss as Pierston's absurd idealizing comes to naught. That is to say, *The Well-Beloved*, chronicling the fall from art into simple sympathetic humanity of its protagonist, is itself very self-consciously a work of art, imposing meaning on the meaningless, and order on the random, while giving value to the specimen, after all. Hardy's full turn to poetry that followed implies a wary but unequivocal affirmation of the value of the lies of consciousness that refuse the limits of mere matter, of the body, and of the stones that constitute Pierston's mythic island, and of the possibility, somehow through art, to intimate compassionately the pains that indifferent nature inflicts on us all individually, as "specimens."

CHAPTER 5

The Poetry of the Novels

This is the wonder of Hardy's novels, and gives them their beauty. The vast, unexplored morality of life itself, what we call the immorality of nature, surrounds us in its eternal incomprehensibility and in its midst goes on the little human morality play

And this is the quality Hardy shares with the great writers ... this setting behind the small action of his protagonists the terrific action of unfathomed nature.

D. H. Lawrence

In the course of this book, I have tried to work through Hardy's more philosophical, if erratic, engagement with large, bleakly interpreted issues, through his often-awkward retreat to respectability, through his preoccupations with the tensions between social class and sexuality, through his aspiration to the ideal that, if it exists, exists beyond the reach of the human, through his obsession with "seeing" and perspective, and, finally, through his commitment to art, where the ideal meets the Darwinian natural world, the tangled bank, and gives it shape. Here is where I wanted to arrive: consideration of the qualities of his prose that emerge from such mixed preoccupations and manage, in spite of all, to feel like a celebration of life in which even Hardy's very dark world is re-enchanted.

Art as a prop against the mindlessness of nature. Form as a defense against its inextricable entanglements. Fiction as exploration that opens on knowledge and the beautiful. However much Hardy's fictions insist on the mind as the creator of meaning, his work always retains that commitment to the reality of the hard unaccommodating world, to its rocklike and permanent and ultimately dominant presence. His recognition of fallibility and limitation that emerges in his concern with vision, and his protective vision of the world through spectacles and windows is not incompatible with his sense of the absolute, adamant reality of the material world, and of nature itself. So Hardy's turn to art is not a turn away from nature or from representation but a powerful sign of engagement with it. It is the means by which his tragic vision incorporates not only fear but love, not only pain but the beautiful, not only passive submission but imaginative exploration.

Despite the sage-like voice of most of his narrators, with the sense they emanate that their vision far transcends the limits of single consciousness, Hardy is always concerned with the "specimen," with ways to see it and feel for it, and with the worlds charged with life that occupy the margins of his protagonists' lives. With vision sharpened by sensitivity to life in all its forms, Hardy persistently describes aspects of Darwin's tangled bank, penetrates and finds shape in its apparent formlessness, and shakes his readers into consciousness of lives beyond story. The perceiver makes way best through that unaccommodating actual by knowing it intimately, precisely – by discovering its peculiarities and thus making peace with it. The best adapted people are those who are at home in the nature they never made but always understand. The art is in the tension between massive entanglement and shaping vision; the love is in the particular. In the midst of disasters and the ruthlessness of natural forces, Hardy's prose bursts into blossom.

This poetic force in the novels is not, certainly, the norm; but, as I have suggested in the Preface, it tends to emerge when the prose is attending to things that the protagonists themselves are not quite noticing, or, noticing, take for granted. Such attention implies the understory that goes on while the characters fail to recognize any apparent relation to the dramas they are in the midst of enacting. I begin with one of the finest examples of this. In *A Pair of Blue Eyes*, which follows the fortunes of Stephen Smith, struggling beyond the class into which he was born, in love with Elfride of the "blue eyes," Stephen faces a crisis. At the point when he comes to realize that he is losing Elfride to his mentor and good friend, Henry Knight, he waits, in dark silence, with "a beating heart," to meet Elfride, who does not appear.

It is apparently a recognizable moment of Victorian drama, if not melodrama, attention focused on the protagonist's desire and frustration and thus on the main lines of the overall story as it is about to turn. But there is a sudden shift of focus: without warning the prose projects to the foreground not what Stephen is feeling but what seems mere background:

> faint sounds only accentuated the silence. The rising and falling of the sea, far away along the coast, was the most important. A minor sound was the scurr of a distant night-hawk. Among the minutest where all were minute were the light settlement of gossamer fragments floating in the air, a toad humbly labouring along through the grass near the entrance, the crackle of

> a dead leaf which a worm was endeavoring to pull into the earth, a waft of
> air, getting nearer and nearer, and expiring at his feet under the burden of
> a winged seed. (*PBE*, ch. 24, pp. 261–262)

What is all this almost inaudible sound doing, so gorgeously, here in the
midst of a Victorian love affair? It is unlikely that Stephen actually hears
the quiet commotion; for him the sounds are part of the silence. But the
experience of reading requires that the reader listen differently, hear the
barely audible, turn eyes from the melodrama to an extraordinarily rich and
complicated nonhuman world. Hardy's narrator hears with almost more
than a naturalist's precision and detail this world of life, and he increases its
volume simply by mentioning it. Stephen's "silence" is, in the larger implications of the scene and the book, almost a symphony of movement and life
going on without the slightest regard for Stephen's unhappy love. Who
outside of Hardy's narrators is going to hear the noise of a worm pulling
a leaf into its hole? Eight years later, Darwin would publish a book demonstrating how the little action that Stephen possibly and Hardy certainly hears
transforms the whole surface of the earth.[1] Does the action make a sound?
Hardy hears it and registers remarkably that all around Stephen there are
processes of regeneration and growth going on, and the seed settles at his
feet. The understory is actually larger than the story.

The revelation of sound is matched one chapter later by revelations of
sight. In a characteristic Hardy moment of spying on unsuspecting figures
in a world where everyone is watching everyone else, Stephen sees Elfride
and Knight together. He watches them step into a summer house, where

> The scratch of a striking light was heard, and a glow radiated from the
> interior of the building. The light gave birth to dancing leaf-shadows, stem-
> shadows, lustrous streaks, dots, sparkles, and threads of silver sheen of all
> imaginable variety and transience. It awakened gnats, which flew upwards to
> it, revealed shiny gossamer threads, disturbed earthworms. Stephen gave
> little attention to these phenomena and less time. He saw in the summer
> house a strongly illuminated picture. (ch. 25, p. 257)

What Stephen sees in that "strongly illuminated picture" is entirely different from what the novel represents: a world that exists in spite of us, that
has nothing to do with us. Yet it is just the world in which our stories
unfold. Hardy transforms a moment almost as extravagantly melodramatic
as the melodrama of *Desperate Remedies* into an extraordinary revelatory
poem about something else. About forms of life that are affected by what
we do, though we don't notice, and about the brilliance and beauty of the
life around us that animates everything.

Hardy's lifelong preoccupation with respectability, with not being touched, with disguising his feelings, is the other side of his unparalleled vision of a world we never made always out there just beyond the limits of our consciousness. His sensitivity to the pervasiveness of overhearing and even spying in a world where everyone is watching everyone else is coincident with his very distinctive powers of observation. Hardy has a sense of the world as a Darwinian plenum, with life and its traces occupying every inch of the world's space, and this sense informs and transforms the stories – ostensibly, and really enough, the focus of his novels. As Virginia Woolf has put it, Hardy's "little prospect of man's existence is ringed by a landscape which, while it exists apart, yet confers a deep and solemn beauty upon his drama" (VW, p. 225). From moment to moment in the novels it presses to the foreground and changes everything.

Through passages such as these, which Woolf notes occur in almost every one of his novels, Hardy transcends their frequent excesses and awkwardness; they make visible the extraordinary secret abundance and connectedness of things, "the terrific action of unfathomable nature." When the novels take their eyes off their stories for an instant, a sentence, a paragraph, they suggest something of the difficulty and the urgency of recognizing and caring for the realities that for the most part we do not see or hear and that therefore seem irrelevant to our lives. They make intuitively comprehensible the tragic, often clunkily schemed fates of the protagonists. Life in Hardy never can or should satisfy the inevitable preoccupations for the self that are the focus of the stories; even the spiders and the gnats and the nighthawks make their demands. Every move we make disturbs other life, earthworms, snails, rabbits, people. Out of the entanglements Hardy makes shapes; his novels persistently see beyond their own stories.

The sense of being watched that this scene arouses is further intensified by Stephen's discovery that there is someone else watching Elfride – someone with her own story, the mother, Mrs. Jethway, of a former lover of Elfride, spying because she believes that Elfride is responsible for her son's death. As often, the Hardy plot clinks and clunks, but the sense of multiple and mutual entanglements makes something memorable of what can sometimes seem contrived melodrama. His acute sense of the existence and reality of others entangled on Darwin's bank creates a powerful understory and moving poetic moments.

I repeat the point I made in the "Preface": Hardy's finest writing is free of those strains of philosophy and high learning that too frequently clog his prose; it is writing that depends on almost uncanny perceptivity of the natural world.[2] Amy King's phrase "reverent form" applies almost perfectly to Hardy's finest writing. She notes that the traditions both of realism and of Victorian realist fiction carry with them, in their minute attention to natural phenomena, reverberations of natural theology, theoretically disposed of by Darwin.[3] The argument might apply well beyond the writers whose reverence is clearly directed at God. The Darwin I have described in an earlier chapter manifests this practice of "reverent form," and so too, I would claim, does Hardy. Such reverence does not entail religious faith in an intelligence capable of producing such extraordinary and beautiful phenomena, but rather implies in its minute attention a sense of the wonders inherent in this world.

II

Passages like those from *A Pair of Blue Eyes* emerge early in Hardy's novel-writing career. They are so intrinsic, despite their poetic intensity, that it is possible to read past them into the narratives that make the novels novels. Moments of extraordinary poetic power, they are, for me at least, the reason Hardy's novels continue to matter beyond any judgment that might be made about his narratives as a whole. They can be read as crystallizations of all the finest elements of his writing and must be seen not as apparently separable pretty parts, but – as Lawrence and Woolf read them – as integral to Hardy's realistic imagination. They are manifestations of Hardy's practice of "reverent form," however painful the vision, however distorted the trees, however indifferent the ephemera are to man's fate. They are the materials through which Hardy's work embraces variations of life beyond the human and makes something beautiful out of the dark realities of the material world and the distortions that social order enforces.

The earliest passage of the sort that attracted my critical attention is the very first paragraph of his second published novel – and his first successful one – *Under the Greenwood Tree*. It is easy to read past it in the rush for story, but it is quietly intrinsic to what follows and, one might add, to the whole range of Hardy's fiction:

> To dwellers in the woods almost every species of tree has its voice as well as its feature. At the passing of the breeze the fir-trees sob and moan no less distinctly than they rock; the holly whistles as it battles with itself; the ash hisses amid its quiverings; the beech rustles while its lace boughs rise and fall. And winter, which modifies the note of such trees as shed their leaves, does not destroy its individuality. (pt. 1, ch. 1, p. 39)

Understated but at the same time breathtaking, the paragraph seems more powerful than the lovely little narrative, the story itself, that follows. The registration of intricacies and particularities of nature is revelatory; but yet more interesting, it immediately raises the question of perspective, for what is registered here is not simply the singularity of the trees, but the remarkable powers of perception of the "dweller in the woods." Here is a piece of that "great background, vital and vivid, which matters more than the people who move upon it" (*P*, p. 419) to which Lawrence alludes. But the people do matter: that they can read nature so finely indicates that they are at home in the world; their perceptions are harmonious with the natural forces among which they live.

The paragraph might be said to announce Hardy's preoccupation with observation of nature, with the powers and subtleties of the natural forces that are at work all the time in his world, and his concern that those rare powers of perception that keep us at home are on the verge of being displaced. The paragraph quietly announces the presence of a world and the powers of understanding it that will frame the novel and the whole Wessex series that Hardy could not at the time have known would be coming.

For the vast majority of Hardy's readers, children of an urban world who do not dwell there, the woods are largely an undifferentiated entanglement of unnamed forms of life. The abrupt nonnarrative opening evokes contrasts and surprises and implies, in the fineness of distinctions made, a way of seeing and hearing that belongs to another sensibility, another culture. Whether or not the paragraph's argument is literally true, its rich play of language gives it a visionary authority: the extravagant truth of the descriptions seems built into the pleasures of the sound, the careful assonances, and the subtly repetitive rhythms. They give shape to a tangle that conventionally trained senses cannot penetrate. The passage as a whole suggests new possibilities of experiencing the world. The wind is no monolith but subtly various forms of sound – sobs, moans, hisses, whistles, rustles; the branches rock or battle with themselves or rise and fall. This is not merely "pretty" writing; it is strong with the energy of Darwinian combat. The wind is an active force and the trees are in constant motion and struggle. Someone is listening very closely to what would otherwise be an undifferentiated whoosh and new possibilities of perception are implied.

In addition, while the paragraph is ostensibly merely descriptive, it is loaded with evaluative implications both in sound and sense. Recognizing the distinctness of each species of tree, not only the shape of its leaves and branches and movements (its "figure") but its whole individualized being in nature, endows each of the trees with a dignity and value that transcend any abstraction and generalization about the "woods." Each of the trees is fully and distinctively alive, even when its leaves are gone. The value applies both to the woods themselves and to the power to perceive them precisely. Individuality requires attention, as does the acuity of perception that reveals that individuality. Their prominence in the first sentences of the novel make it difficult to dismiss the trees, or the wind, as pretty background.

And yet the paragraph does nothing to advance a story, which turns out to be the love affair between Dick Dewy and Fancy Day. If the paragraph were omitted in a reprint, no new reader would notice. At the same time, the fact that the dweller in the woods has found a way to be at home in the world of tangled banks is crucial to the novel's development. One might even say that the struggle to make oneself at home in the world is central to the work of all of Hardy's fiction: being at home is a relatively rare condition. Hardy's famous preoccupation with the death of a rural and agrarian culture whispers through these trees without overt articulation, just as it is thematically central to the story of Dick and Fancy. Even more important than the coming loss of the woods is the possibility of loss of the powers of perception that allow people to live comfortably among them.

Lingering over the first paragraph as the narrative itself refuses to do in its rapid movement to story, we can better appreciate the nonnarrative (Hardy would have been pleased to have it called "poetic") strength of his writing. In the paragraph, with the benefit of retrospect and foresight, it is possible to detect many of those qualities that give to Hardy his distinction and greatness as a writer. Latent in it is the self-conscious artist Hardy, the kinder gentler (if ever nervously somber) narrator, who quietly loves the life (or at least the individuals who embody it) about which he tells such sad tales. But it is also the Hardy who, however gentle, registers with cold and often ironic clarity the activities in nature that entail "battle," as the branches of the holly battle with themselves, as the wind relentlessly rushes through the trees, as the trees work out their lives regardless of human need or desire. It is the Hardy who reads Darwin's darkest messages as provocation for almost universal love of living things, the Hardy for whom the world is thick with meaning that is legible to the observant eye.

The morality of the life with which Hardy surrounds his characters may be "unexplored," as Lawrence puts it, but the world of that life is knowable, and every object signifies. If you hear a rustle in the wind, you know it is a beech tree; if you hear a whistle in the wind, you know it is a holly. It is just Hardy's power to recognize the peculiarities, particularities, and distinctness of life that creates the sense Lawrence emphasizes – life remains outside the range of human rationality and science. The more forcefully Hardy demonstrates the knowability of objects we usually do not notice, the more significant and urgent they become, the less they seem compatible with the social conventions that are designed to tame them.

Once again, here is the Hardy for whom all the world is constantly observed and all secrets eventually revealed, the Hardy who stands back, observingly, from observing eyes and unearthed meanings, and who works out complicated strategies to evade exposure. Hardy the narrator hides behind "the dweller in the woods," but, as the paragraph makes clear, sees with just the precision and sensitivity attributed to that "dweller." Implicit too is the Hardy who values and laments the incompatibility of human desire and mind and sensibility with the ways of nature that these reveal. There also, finally, is the anti-realist Hardy who, within a recognizably realist mode, claims that his work is only a set of "seemings," patterns in a complexly woven carpet. The revelatory quality of the paragraph, derived from the hypersensitive registration of sounds and differences, moves beyond realism to "reverent form."

Given the widespread critical perception that Hardy almost always narrates a world that is both inscrutable and philosophically inconsistent, it seems to me of the first importance to recognize that his world, as in this paragraph, is nevertheless almost entirely knowable. Dwellers in the woods can read it and by reading it survive in it. Non-natives, like Mrs. Charmond of *The Woodlanders*, would not be able to distinguish the voices of the winds, and she cannot find her way alone out of the woods. The woods will indeed destroy those who enter them having lost their "woods-dwelling" instincts to the conventions of society and morality and education. With only social conventions as a guide, you will get lost. Part of what can be known about the woods is that they operate on "natural" principles, according to the processes of natural selection and of physics. The "unexplored morality" of which Lawrence writes is the sheer natural energy that drives all living things. What can be known about them is that their ways are not those of the societies that are displacing them. The problem is not that the woods and the world can't be understood but that many people, perhaps the very readers of the novels – displaced, urbanized, deracinated, self-preoccupied, merely unobservant – fail to read. Against the tide of time and history, Hardy's prose struggles to revivify the power to recognize the varieties of life in nature and make such fine distinctions.

It is a Darwinian project, after all, and in Hardy's world as in Darwin's, there is always the "rastro," the trail, the track – the mark all things leave of their history. Everything in Darwin exists in time and is fully knowable only through the history whose traces it leaves. Hardy's world, like Darwin's, is overabundant with such tracks, not only, for example, in the famous fossils into whose faces the perilously dangling Henry Knight looks, but also, in *The Woodlanders*, in Grace's footstep in the mud that Mr. Melbury preserves after Grace leaves home for school (not to speak of the past that is built into the aches and pains that Farmer Melbury feels), or in the light of the stars that Swithin observes millennia after they radiate it, or, as in *Return of the Native* on Egdon Heath, "the finger touches of the last geological change"(*RN*, ch. 1, p. 56) or in the traditional music that the Mellstock parish choir make, or in the sound of the wind through the leaves. There is a story behind every object, history bulges from stones, from sounds, from movements. The beauty of the life and movement, even when it is signifying nature's indifference and hostility, is evident, and the novels regularly indulge the excitement not only of hearing and seeing minutiae but of understanding how they will develop when our eyes are turned away or how they got there in the first place.

Like the little sketch Hardy drew of the eweleaze, with his spectacles observing and distorting the scene, *Under the Greenwood Tree* (like most of his novels) gives even to the parts of the world that we are likely to take for granted or not even notice a life and individuality that requires attention and a feeling that might be taken as love.

Throughout the novel, as it pursues the simple and comically shaped plot line by which Dick and Fancy come together in marriage, the world implied by the wind in the branches of the first paragraph, "the terrific action of unfathomed nature," surrounds the action. This other life persists on the edges and reemerges ironically in the slightly qualified comic ending. It is noted in the lovely pastoral opening to the chapter describing the marriage of Dick and Fancy ("pathetic fallacy," one might call it), reaffirming the importance to the story of the Lawrentian world that does not, like the first paragraph, officially participate in the narrative but that surrounds it:

> The last day of the story is dated just subsequent to that point in the development of the seasons when country people go to bed among nearly naked trees, are lulled to sleep by a fall of rain, and awake next morning among green ones; when the landscape appears embarrassed with the sudden weight and brilliancy of its leaves; when the night-jar comes and strikes up for the summer his tune of one note; when the apple-trees have blossomed and

the roads and orchard-grass become spotted with fallen petals; when the faces of the delicate flowers are darkened and their heads weighted down by the throng of honey bees, which increase their humming till humming is too mild a term for the all-pervading sound; and when cuckoos, blackbirds, and sparrows, that have hitherto been merry and respectful neighbours, become noisy and persistent intimates. (pt. 5, ch. 1, p. 209).

This is a far gentler, more generalized, and more "literary" paragraph than the book's opening, but its confident representation of a whole series of symptoms of early spring registers again the presence of a world far beyond the range of the story. Despite its far greater acquiescence in popular spring images, it too marks the presence of a nonhuman world. Like the opening paragraph, it registers a life that surrounds story, and implies an energy that transcends it.

But while this paragraph only gently intimates a tension between the human life and "life" itself, the novel's conclusion gets much closer to the sort of disparity between convention and life implied in its first paragraph. Dick Dewy is confident that his happiness in having married Fancy Day is built on the fact that "there is such full confidence between us." "We have no secrets from each other," Dick says, to which Fancy slyly responds, "none from today," and on the instant there comes "a loud, musical, and liquid voice – Come hither. Come hither. Come hither.'" The wild and fantastically varied song of the nightingale fighting for his space and luring females is the reality behind the conventional marriage plot. Fancy reacts to the call and concludes the book: "'Oh 'tis the nightingale,' murmured she, and thought of a secret she would never tell" (pt. 5, ch. 2, p. 226).

This is, certainly, cute, and hardly tragic, but the line does invoke "Life's Little Ironies" that became so much the subject of Hardy's poems and was always central to his narratives. The intimation of Hardy's darker novels is latent, if only minimally intimated, here. The Nightingale calls out of traditions of poetry that invoke romance and raptures, but not as a way to romanticize the marriage, rather as a counterpoint to it. Despite its role in undercutting Dick's naïve trust, Hardy's nightingale does true nightingale work and is not really a romantic symbol. While the song is described as "liquid" and "musical," the nightingale's voice is wild and sexual – Tippiwit! Swe-e-et! Ki-ki-ki! – almost comically various and crude. The bird inhabits a world beyond the limits of decorum to which Fancy has, perhaps reluctantly, committed herself. It is an almost insanely various and vociferous singer as it stakes its claim to its mating spot, but it is also a skulker and calls out of a "neighboring thicket," not visible (as nightingales only rarely are). Remaining in a comic, ironic mode, Hardy invokes another, an indecorous world. The nightingale points to that world of natural energy that so often forms the understory of Hardy's great novels.

III

Return of the Native, the earliest of Hardy's books to manifest that tragic vision which we now take as characteristic of his work, is also full of passages in which the understory of nonhuman life manifests itself. In its fictional world, as Penny Boumelha has put it, "the daylight plot of familiar social interaction . . . is shadowed by something stranger" (Boumelha, 257). While much of the book suffers from some of the excesses of Hardy's ponderous style, much also evokes richly imagined worlds that bring the narrative to pause. The narrative drive itself gives way to the world that is the condition for the story's unfolding. In a pattern that by now should be familiar, the novel plays out tensions between limiting convention (most conspicuously again, marriage) and natural energies; once again, also, it dramatizes the displacement of tradition, in figures like those of the Mellstock choir. Yet its most powerful effects emerge not in the brooding philosophical voice of the narrator but in the engagement with the understory juxtaposed to the very particularly imagined lives of the individual characters.

This is striking enough in the famous, over-portentous opening description of Egdon Heath. But a better sense of the quality of the writing and the pervasiveness and significance of that "something stranger" can be drawn from what I take to be the most effective and dramatically powerful sequence in the novel – the record of the pilgrimage and return of Mrs. Yeobright, seeking reconciliation with her son and finding, exhausted and defeated, death. Mrs. Yeobright takes center stage in a novel that could be more conventionally read as a rather melodramatic love story, between Clym and Eustacia. But Mrs. Yeobright is the focus for an extended sequence, the only "plot" element of which is the fact that she dies, and dies disheartened and disillusioned.

Mrs. Yeobright matters, and so too does the world into which she expires. At each stage of her pilgrimage, the novel registers, largely through her eyes, abundant and various forms of life. On the way to Clym's house,

> Occasionally she came to a spot where independent worlds of ephemerons were passing their time in mad carousal, some in the air, some on the hot

ground and vegetation, some in the tepid and stringy water of a nearly dried pool. All the shallower ponds had decreased to a vaporous mud amid which the maggoty shapes of innumerable obscure creatures could be indistinctly seen, heaving and wallowing with enjoyment. (pt. IV, ch. 3, p. 338)

The revulsion implied by the prose is countered by the keenness of the observations it allows; what matters most is the life itself, surviving in unlikely places as summer dries out the landscape. Whatever befalls Hardy's characters, they are surrounded by a world recognizable in Darwin's prose, one in which life, however embattled, flourishes anywhere. "Well may we affirm," says Darwin, "that every part of the world is habitable!" He lists unlikely places – "lakes of brine," "cavernous" sub-volcanic waters, "warm mineral springs," the ocean, "the upper regions of the atmosphere," "the surface of perpetual snow." All, he says, "support organic beings."[4] Such unexpected life turns up again on the brutal summer day of Mrs. Yeobright's final defeated walk, even when "all visible animation disappeared from the landscape." The minutely crowded land-scape becomes, as so often in Hardy, an ironic counterpoint to the protagonist's condition – the happiness of those distinctly nonhuman creatures contrasts sharply with her mood and mission. Concerned as the reader must be at this point with the fate of Mrs. Yeobright, the foreground becomes these "independent worlds" that exist regardless of her trials, regardless of her physical weakness, regardless of the complications of her thought and feeling. The story of the Yeobrights becomes only a very small part of the living world; these tiny organisms, untroubled by the oedipal crises of human relationships, thrive in what to human perception is mere mud and mess, "maggoty," ugly shapes, abundant, busy at what they do, not philosophizing.

The integration of the understory with the main one becomes evident when Mrs. Yeobright sees a furze cutter who, in his activities, "seemed to be of no more account in life than an insect . . . a mere parasite of the heath" (pt IV, ch. 5, p. 339). But this mere parasite is slowly individuated: it is the son she has been seeking, and the denigrating perception of the furze cutter as merely a member of a natural class, like the insects, is transformed in her recognition that he (implicitly like all furze-cutters) has his own peculiar way of walking. The insect world, like the sounds of the trees in the wind in *Under the Greenwood Tree*, is individuated; the life merely categorized and dismissed becomes quite another thing, something that matters, some-thing relevant to the observer. The process that Mrs. Yeobright undergoes is the process of Hardy's prose itself.

Here Hardy's psychology, in keeping with his persistent strategy of not entering deeply into the minds of his characters in modernist mode, is played out for the most part outside the mind, in the "objective" rendition of things, in the careful description of the way people act and react to the external world. Meaning is to be inferred from the traces, out of which a deep past is constructed. Mrs. Yeobright's relation to the insect nature of her son unleashes a psychological drama that can't be played out in Jamesian mode; the Lawrentian irrational is at work.

The power of nature ironically reasserts itself immediately after Mrs. Yeobright thinks about how she might save her son from absorption into nature. Taking a fatigued break from her mission, she sits amid a group of nine trees, "singularly battered, rude, and wild," among which "not a bough ... but was splintered, looped, and distorted by the fierce weather that there held them at its mercy whenever it prevailed":

> Some were blasted and split as if by lightning, black stains as from fire marking their sides, while the ground at their feet was strewn with dead fir-needles and heaps of cones blown down in the gales of past years, ... On the present afternoon, when no perceptible wind was blowing, the trees kept up a perpetual moan which one could hardly believe to be caused by the air. (pt IV, ch. 5, p. 340)

While it is tempting to take the scene as a metaphor for Mrs. Yeobright's state of mind, it is yet more importantly just what it is represented to be – a vital yet painful world, not of ephemerons, but of trees, not of happy maggoty mud insects, but of life persisting and bending under the force of nature that works indifferently on human and all living creatures. It is another chapter in the understory.

Yet another chapter of that understory unfolds on Mrs. Yeobright's return. Mistakenly thinking that her son has barred the door to her, she turns away, devastated, late in a burning hot afternoon, like "a woman who was now no less anxious to escape from the scene than she had previously been to enter it" (pt IV, ch. 6, p. 348). Exhausted both physically and psychologically, Mrs. Yeobright "continued to creep along in short stages with long breaks" with sun directly in her face, "like some merciless incendiary, brand in hand, waiting to consume her" (pt. IV, ch. 6, p. 351).

And on her return, when "all visible animation disappeared from the landscape," there came "the intermittent husky notes of the male grass-hoppers from every tuft of furze," sign "that amid the prostration of the larger animal species an unseen insect world was busy in all the fullness of life" (pt IV, ch. 6, p. 351). There is the "objective" Hardy, with the qualifier "male" offering a distinctively Hardyan touch. Inside Mrs. Yeobright's pain we yet hear the sounds of the grasshoppers punctuating the silence, and that sound marks an understory: only the male grasshopper calls, and almost always for the purpose of attracting a mate. As Mrs. Yeobright moves to death, the grasshoppers are affirming life. The juxtaposition here, as in other such passages, is not merely, if at all, ironic. It is one of those moments to which Woolf refers when she claims that Hardy's novels create "the sense that the little prospect of man's existence is ringed by a landscape which, while it exists apart, yet confers a deep and solemn beauty upon his drama."

Hardy's objective method persists to the very point of death. Hopelessly fatigued, battered by the hostile sun, Mrs. Yeobright finally sits down:

> In front of her a colony of ants had established a thoroughfare across the way, where they toiled a never-ending and heavy-laden throng. To look down upon them was like observing a city street from the top of a tower. She remembered that this bustle of ants had been in progress for years at the same spot – doubtless those of the old times were the ancestors of these which walked there now. She leant back to obtain more thorough rest, and the soft eastern portion of the sky was as great a relief to her eyes as the thyme was to her head. While she looked a heron arose on that side of the sky and flew on with his face toward the sun. He had come dripping wet from some pool in the valleys, and as he flew the edges and lining of his wings, his thighs and his breast were so caught by the bright sunbeams that he appeared as if formed of burnished silver. (pt IV, ch. 6, p. 351)

Life indifferently continues as Mrs. Yeobright lies dying, but the affect is strikingly different from that of the bitterly ironic scene of Jude's death, when the festival in the streets below his window carries on. In the midst of Mrs. Yeobright's pilgrimage to death, life in all its plenitude emerges, not abstractly, as a kind of official affirmation that, yes, the world is full of life, but with a particularity that, while it often implies irony, almost always also implies a marvelous vitality that survives even the worst of human failures. As Mrs. Yeobright dies, there remains the inferred "pool in the valley," and the remarkable design the language makes out of the sun illuminating the chance emergence of the heron, outlined in silver as it soars. It is possible to reduce this passage to a symbolic expression of Mrs. Yeobright's longing for death and escape from betrayal and loss, since the bird moves up "away from all contact with the earthly ball to which she was pinioned; and she wished she could arise uncrushed from its surface as he flew then." But to reduce this striking moment, with its brilliantly defined heron and a city of ants, to mere symbol is to lose just what distinguishes Hardy's ambivalent relation to the natural world. Fullness can be the consequence of his pages, even as they sink into darkness.

But Clym joins the ants and the twisted trees and the maggots and the ephemera that Mrs. Yeobright has encountered on her pilgrimage. The ants, in their tininess, affirm a long independent history; the heron in its glistening flight affirms the possibility of a natural future. The ephemera, all those creatures that last for so short a time, belong to a history of life that can be traced deep into the past and that will, this kind of writing intimates, outlast the more extended dramas of human suffering and alienation from their world. Mrs. Yeobright and the narrator have minds and sensibilities apparently incompatible with the natural energies of the world they are incongruously empowered to recognize and describe. The pathos of that recognition is a large part of the stories that Hardy tells; the presence of that vital world intensifies the compassion of the prose for the humans who live so ambivalently inside and outside it. As vulnerable as the ephemera, they, unlike the ephemera, know their vulnerability; they know also how beautiful the silvered wings of the heron can be.

IV

It is not only gnats and worms, nighthawks and herons – for Hardy, the world beyond the focus of his protagonists (and of us in our daily lives) extends with at least equal richness to the stars and the cosmos. That larger world surrounds us, shapes us, counterpoints with our little stories, just as the ephemera do, and knowing how to see it, as the dwellers in the woods know, is a skill that makes it possible to feel at ease in this Darwinian world we never made. It is, however, another characteristically paradoxical Hardyan condition – at once a way to the fullness that is the object of Hardy's reverent form, and a radical reminder of the insignificance of human life in relation to the whole living busy world. If the presence of hitherto unnoticed ephemera emphasizes that insignificance, then imagine what the presence of stars might do.

The Hardy novel that most obviously engages that macro-world and its power to diminish the human is *Two on a Tower*. The stars are normally only slightly more often the focus of human attention than the ephemera illuminated during Stephen's crisis of love. And yet, while the novel insists on the overwhelming reality of a world infinitely larger than anything human, it also emphasizes an aspect of Hardy's "objectivity" as narrator that rarely surfaces so directly and simply: the stars are overwhelming, the empty spaces insupportable on the human scale, but knowing their reality and the alternative form of life and being that they represent is, in the end, less important than any individual human being who lives under them. The passion for seeing other worlds is set directly in contrast with human compassion and love. The tension makes the novel, which might be seen to drift away into Victorian melodrama after its very strong beginning, and reveals much about what Hardy is up to everywhere in his fiction.

Early in the novel, Swithin allows Lady Constantine to look through his telescope, although he warns her that what she will see through it can be terrifying. "Magnitude," he tells Lady Constantine, "which up to a certain point has grandeur, has beyond it ghastliness." Out there lies "a vast formless something that reveals very little of itself" (*TT*, ch. 8, p. 96). Science struggles to make order out of that mass; Hardy's art in representing it has a similar object, but it can do that only by focusing as much on the act of perception, and the felt implication of that perception for the actors behind it as on the sidereal phenomena themselves:

> the interest of their sidereal observations led them on, till the knowledge that scarce any other human vision was traveling within a hundred million miles of their own gave them such a sense of the isolation of that faculty as almost to be a sense of isolation in respect of their whole personality, causing a shudder at its absoluteness. At night, when human discords and harmonies are hushed, in a general sense, for the greater part of twelve hours, there is nothing to moderate the blow with which the infinitely great, the stellar universe, strikes down upon the infinitely little, the mind of the beholder; and this was the case now. Having got closer to immensity than their fellow-creatures, they saw at once its beauty and its frightfulness. They more and more felt the contrast between their own tiny magnitudes and those among which they had recklessly plunged, till they were oppressed with the presence of a vastness they could not cope with even as an idea, and which hung about them like a nightmare. (*TT*, ch. 9, pp. 86–87)

Hardy was well versed in the problems of perception in astronomy, the degree to which the reading of the stars was inflected by the viewers' positions and the movement of the earth on which they stand.[5] Every perception is singular; multiple perceptions cross and contradict even as they are being as objective as possible. Here the usual subtexts of Hardy's work become the texts: everything depends on powers of perception, the point of view of the perceivers, and the juxtaposition of the seeing eye and the feeling spirit with the extremes of the natural world. As Swithin gets absorbed in that magnitude, the story returns bearing the implications of the scene: "I fear," says Lady Constantine, "that I have put into your hands an instrument to effect my own annihilation" (ch. 8, p. 87). Swithin, like

Hardy, is deep in the work of making sense of the unfathomable, of giving it a shape.

He is developing a "theory" (which he soon will publish and that will lead to his professionalization and his departure from Lady Constantine). In self-consciously and overtly juxtaposing the vast natural world to the little love story, Hardy gives that ghastly and enormous world a shape as well. It is a pre-rocket space probe – the imagination of what it means to see into space, to travel millions of miles with the eye, and then to return to the little realities of earth ("Do come out of it," Lady Constantine coaxes the long-silent Swithin). The wonder is that the little eye takes in the vastness, as the little human brain incongruously achieves imaginations of vastness for which it was never constructed.

But that wonder takes second place in *Two on a Tower* to the incongruity. More important, the counterpoint to space travel in Lady Constantine's quite personal response, shifting from space to "me," suggests that the hundreds of millions of miles do not, after all, count as much as the little lives and love affair of the protagonists. The plot of *Two on a Tower* also clinks and clunks on its way to something like tragedy, but it does so by assimilating the scientific knowledge, Hardy's always acute perception of what's out there, to the little actions of Victorian melodrama.[6] Objectivity and human need and limitation play off against each other in Swithin's work and Lady Constantine's sympathetic and then loving support. While the novel's drama is in the love affair and not in outer space, no work of Hardy's makes more clear the tension between the objective/real and the ideal, of the difficulty of disentangling them, of the degree to which the nonhuman world runs in counterpoint to the human and ultimately determines the shape it will take. As Gossin has put it, "Hardy, as he wrote his novels, was always already a *poet*" (p. 228).

Swithin's obsession with the other worlds of space leads him far from Lady Constantine, both physically and morally. His scientific obsession (as in a tradition that runs from *Dr. Faustus*, through *Frankenstein* and, let's say, *Godzilla* and *Jurassic Park*) loses sight of the simply human. Swithin, however, is no native of the skies as the dwellers in the woods are native among the various trees that no alien would recognize. In a prose reminiscent of the experience of Stephen Smith among the suddenly lit ephemera, he traces Swithin's work

> in regions revealed only to the instrumental observer, were suns of hybrid kind – fire-fogs, floating nuclei, globes that flew in groups like swarms of

bees, and other extraordinary sights – which, when decomposed by Swithin's equatorial, turned out to be the beginning of a new series of phenomena instead of the end of an old one.

There were gloomy deserts in those southern skies such as the north shows scarcely an example of; sites set apart for the position of suns which for some unfathomable reason were left uncreated, their places remaining ever since conspicuous by their emptiness.

The inspection of those chasms brought him a second pulsation of that old horror which he had used to describe to Viviette as produced in him by the bottomlessness in the north heaven. The ghostly finger of limitless vacancy touched him now on the other side. Infinite deeps in the north stellar region had a homely familiarity about them, when compared with the infinite deeps in the region of the South Pole. This was an even more unknown tract of the unknown. Space here, being less the historic haunt of human thought than overhead at home, seemed to be pervaded with a more lonely loneliness ... In these experiments with tubes and glasses, important as they were to human intellect, there was little food for the sympathetic instincts which create the changes in life. (ch. 41, pp. 280–281)

Swithin's explorations are those of an alien exploring worlds they never made. The language with which the book renders his perceptions forces upon readers a sense of alienation, but is itself a form of coping with that alienation and making the "ghostly" beautiful.

In registering Swithin's perceptions and feelings about the extra-human world, I am not claiming that the kinder, gentler Hardy whom I have been trying to evoke is ever conventionally happy with the ways of the world – it is both terrifying and beautiful. The incompatibility between the enormous and vital worlds that surround his little dramas and the vital Lawrentian worlds I have been affirming is too strong a part of his imagination to be transformed into optimism. It is something larger than optimism or pessimism, sometimes emphasizing the terror, sometimes the beauty.

In *Far from the Madding Crowd*, for example, a sense of the vastness of the universe produces quite other effects. The world of the stars that encloses our own, that counterpoints the human stories, is registered not as alien, but with a feeling that might be called reverence. Here the formless vital world takes humanly compatible shape after all; the tangled bank becomes intelligible, and a means to human satisfaction. The book intimates the possibility, as Gossin has put it, that Hardy's reading of science "yielded some slight possibility that conscious life could fit itself to the environment to better fit itself ... and could also encourage each of us to try to better fit ourselves and each other, both materially and psychologically, to the realities around us" (p. 231). But knowing both the large and the small so as to be at home in the world like the wood-dwellers in *Under the Greenwood Tree* requires a radical shift of attention away from the self. The experience of fullness comes in those rare moments when the self is displaced, and even then there are no guarantees.

One cannot feel cozy in the sublime, and in Hardy we have seen that there is a negative sublime, a finely drawn representation of the myriad activities of nature that are ugly or dangerous or repulsive to humans, but that emerge on the page with poetic force. In the long run, fictional narrative only confirms what we unselfconsciously feel, our own centrality. But Hardy's narratives discover worlds that humble us, that force changes in perspective, that extend feelings beyond the limits of immediate perception. His genius and originality in "physical perception" take him beyond the inevitable egoism of conventional narrative into new imaginations of possible modes of human satisfaction.

Far from the Madding Crowd moves from the alternative worlds that we have seen evoked in *A Pair of Blue Eyes* and *Under the Greenwood Tree* to the vast spaces of *Two on a Tower*. At each place in this movement, Hardy finds a language of more than accommodation. There is an echo, for example, of the first paragraph of *Under the Greenwood Tree* in this passage:

> The thin grasses more or less coating the hill were touched by the wind in breezes of differing powers, and almost of differing natures – one rubbing the blades heavily, another taking them piercingly, another brushing them like a soft broom. The instinctive act of humankind was to stand and listen and learn how the trees on the right and trees on the left wailed or chaunted to each other in the regular antiphonies of a cathedral choir; how hedges and other shapes to leeward then caught the note, lowering it to the tenderest sob; and how the hurrying gust then plunged into the south, to be heard no more. (*FMC*, ch. 2, p. 9)[7]

The comparison of the sounds of the wind to the "regular antiphonies of a cathedral choir" is a clear manifestation of that tendency to secular enchantment or reverent form that runs as a bass note through most of the darkest of Hardy's narratives. But once again, the poetic power is in the minute attention to the textures of experience, and interestingly, the power is not noted as exceptional, but as "the instinctive act of humankind," an instinct that now requires, in the hands of the novelist, the most severe poetic discipline of precise observation. The capacity to distinguish the sounds of the wind should be second nature. A return to that nature – learning to read the physical world, to understand and value its traces, learning to individuate – is a condition for caring for the individual.

Learning to see and thus to feel – these are essential objectives of Hardy's art. In passages such as these Hardy's mirror of nature becomes a lamp, a revelation of how the entanglements of the world can be perceived so as to give them human significance. Such passages startle with a shock of recognition, revealing complexities one had perhaps intuited but had never troubled to recognize before. The shock is partly in the revelation of the hitherto unnoticed beauty inherent in the entanglements of nature.

Gabriel Oak, who among Hardy's protagonists comes the closest to being allowed a happy ending with a woman he desires (though he knows he has been second best to Bathsheba), manages only because he has unsentimentally come to terms with the nature on which his living has always depended. He accepts the conditions of the life that nature, chance, and social constraints have imposed upon him, but he thoroughly understands those terms, understands the vital alternative lives that surge through the natural world.

Through the consciousness of Oak, Hardy's prose extends perception of particulars through the whole universe of living things. The language has a precision recognizably Hardyan and recognizably revelatory. In one stunning passage, Hardy celebrates with unusual good feeling the capacity of the human mind to know and participate in the vast indifferent world that Swithin and Lady Constantine experience as "ghastly." Oak does not need a telescope or a theory of astronomy to recognize the "parallax" at work. He feels the earth move under him as the stars move around him.

The quality of enchantment here expands from ephemera to stars:

> The roll of the world eastward is almost a palpable movement. The sensation may be caused by the panoramic glide of the stars past earthly objects, which is perceptible in a few minutes of stillness, or by the better outlook upon space that a hill affords, or by the wind, or by the solitude; but whatever be its origin, the impression of riding along is vivid and abiding. The poetry of motion is a phrase much in use, and to enjoy the epic form of that gratification it is necessary to stand on a hill at a small hour of the night, and, having first expanded with a sense of difference from the mass of civilised mankind, who are dreamwrapped and disregardful of all such proceedings at this time, long and quietly watch your stately progress through the stars. After a nocturnal reconnoiter it is hard to get back to earth, and to believe that the consciousness of such majestic speeding is derived from a tiny human frame. (ch. 2, p. 9)

Here is another lesson in observation, this time almost explicitly educative. The language is generalized before it moves to Oak, who is at this moment experiencing what the narrator has just described impersonally.

Again, Hardy emphasizes the failures of attention that this writing corrects. While Oak feels the movement of earth and sky, most people are "dream-wrapped." However wonderful the experience of the passage through the stars may be, yet more astonishing is the power of human consciousness, locked though it is in "a tiny human frame."

When in the depth of night Gabriel is out on that hill from which, the narrator says, one can observe and actually feel the stately movements of the heavens, he "stood still after looking at the sky as a useful instrument, and regarded it in an appreciative spirit, as a work of art superlatively beautiful" (ch. 2, p. 12). A work of art produced by mindless processes. But a work of art in that this tiny human consciousness has been able to assimilate and understand it.

In her remarkable book *H Is for Hawk*, Helen MacDonald summarizes the effect of her extreme and passionate training of a goshawk she called "Mabel," which she had undertaken as a way of dealing with the overwhelming grief she was experiencing at the death of her father. There in her reality was the Hardyan darkness to despair, and there in Mabel, that ferocious nonhuman predator, she found a way back into life. The effects MacDonald describes seem to me almost precisely those that the experience of engaging the poetry of Hardy's novel produces.

> Of all the lessons I've learned in my months with Mabel this is the greatest of all: that there is a world of things out there – rocks and trees and stones and grass and all the things that crawl and run and fly. They are all things in themselves, but we make them sensible to us by giving them meanings that shore up our own views of the world. In my time with Mabel I've learned how you feel more human once you have known, even in your imagination, what it is like to be not. And I have learned, too, the danger that comes in mistaking the wildness we give a thing for the wildness that animates it. Goshawks are things of death and blood and gore, but they are not excuses for atrocities. Their inhumanity is to be treasured because what they do has nothing to do with us at all.[8]

Here is Hardy's understory sense of the overwhelming and beautiful reality of the nonhuman world, and here, in MacDonald's experience, is that decentering of self, that shifting of focus from ego to the lives of other beings; and here is the writer's recognition of the way mind and art transform the nonhuman into meaning; and finally, here is the implication of love in the midst of ferocity. The ephemera, the heron, the stars and trees and wind about which Hardy writes are what they are, not what we imagine them, and have nothing to do with us at all – and yet everything.

So Hardy's poetry within the novels, even when it registers the ghastly and grotesque, opens on the imagination of a healthy and life-giving relation to a natural world utterly indifferent and never entirely knowable: "the art," as I have already quoted Hardy as saying, "lies in making these defects the basis of a hitherto unperceived beauty." It pushes toward a recognition of the centrality and importance of our powers of perception, and is sensitive to the consequences of such intense attention. Listening for the wind in the trees, feeling the movement of the earth under one's feet and against the stars, and recognizing the history of ants and the abundance of life forms beyond our normal vision become means to "fullness," to being at home in a world that in its vastness can be ghastly, in its constant struggles for life can be vicious and cruel, and in its utter materiality excludes the possibility of a divine consciousness overseeing all. Hardy's prose, opening the understory that is the condition for the lives it narrates, makes aesthetic sense of so difficult a world, explores by way of "objective" vision the possibilities and irrationalities of consciousness itself, and translates mindless nature, through extraordinary alertness to the particulars of the natural world, into a humane and beautiful art.

Notes

Preface

1. For a leading example of this, see Elaine Showalter's essay on *The Mayor of Casterbridge*, in *Critical Approaches to the Fiction of Thomas Hardy*, ed. Dale Kramer (London: Macmillan Press, 1979), p. 99.
2. In an essay with much relevance to my arguments here, William A. Cohen notes how what he used to think of as "the boring parts," the nonnarrative parts of the novels, are generally talked of by critics as their "poetry." But he insists – and this is part of the burden of this book – those boring parts are critical to the way Hardy imagines the world, where the material world flows through "nature" (a human idea), in which Hardy includes the human. The distinction between nature out there and the humans in here becomes artificial in Hardy. See W. A. Cohen, "Arborealities: The Tactile Ecology of Hardy's Woodlanders," *Interdisciplinary Studies in the Long Nineteenth Century*, 19 (2014), DoI: http//dx.dit.org/10.16995/ntn.690.
3. Gillian Beer, *Darwin's Plots: Evolutionary Narrative in Darwin, George Eliot, and Nineteenth-Century Fiction* (London: Routledge and Kegan Paul, 1983), p. 241.
4. George Levine, *Darwin Loves You: Natural Selection and the Reenchantment of the World* (Princeton: Princeton University Press, 2006).
5. For a useful consideration of the importance of Lawrence in Hardy criticism, see Michael Herbert, "Lawrence's Hardy," in Phillip Mallett, ed., *Thomas Hardy in Context* (Cambridge: Cambridge University Press, 2013), pp. 449–458.
6. See, among many others, for example, Peter Widdowson, *On Thomas Hardy: Late Essays and Earlier* (London; Macmillan Press, Ltd., 1998); Roger Ebbatson, *Hardy: The Margin of the Unexpressed* (Sheffield: Sheffield Academic Press, 1993); Lance St. John Butler, ed., *Alternative Hardy* (New York: St. Martin's Press, 1989); Simon Gattrell, *Hardy the Creator: A Textual Biography* (Oxford: Clarendon Press, 1988).
7. George Eliot, *Middlemarch* (Oxford: Oxford University Press, 1998 [1872]), ch. xx, p. 192.

1 Shaping Hardy's Art

1. John Bayley, *An Essay on Hardy* (Cambridge: Cambridge University Press, 1978), p. 31.
2. Tom Paulin, *Thomas Hardy: The Poetry of Perception* (London: Palgrave Macmillan, 1966), p. 25.
3. Thomas Hardy, *The Collected Poems of Thomas Hardy* (London: Macmillan, 1952), pp. 62–63.

2 Hardy and Darwin

1. In the first edition of Darwin's *On the Origin of Species*, he uses the word "wonder" a half dozen times. Things or actions are described as "wonderful" or "wonderfully" at least 35 times.
2. Penny Boumelha, " 'Wild Regions of Obscurity,': Narrative in *The Return of the Native*," in Keith Wilson, ed., *A Companion to Thomas Hardy* (Chichester: Wiley/Blackwell, 2009), p. 256.
3. A. Dwight Culler, "The Darwinian Revolution and Literary Form," in George Levine and William Madden, eds., *The Art of Victorian Prose* (New York: Oxford University Press, 1968), p. 225.
4. To be scientifically respectable, Darwin had to exclude chance from the workings of nature, and yet his theory seems to demonstrate the chance development of the many forms of life. Natural selection is a stochastic process. The complications are explored in interesting detail in Curtis Johnson, *Darwin's Dice: The Idea of Chance in the Thought of Charles Darwin* (Oxford: Oxford University Press, 2015).
5. Janet Browne, *Charles Darwin: The Origin and After – the Years of Fame* (New York: Alfred A. Knopf, 2002), p. 460.
6. Taylor's monumental *A Secular Age* (Cambridge, MA: Harvard University Press, 2007) opens with a discussion of "fullness." See also Jane Bennett, *The Enchantment of Modern Life: Attachments, Crossings, Ethics* (Princeton: Princeton University Press, 2001).
7. See her forthcoming "The Divine Commonplace: Natural History, the Theology of Nature, and the Novel."
8. George Levine, *Darwin Loves You: Natural Selection and the Re-enchantment of the World* (Princeton: Princeton University Press, 2006).
9. See also Jane Bennett, *The Enchantment of Modern Life*, p. 4.
10. See Max Weber, "Science as a Vocation," in H. H. Gerth and C. Wright Mills, eds., *From Max Weber: Essays in Sociology* (New York: Oxford University Press, 1971).
11. Robert Richards, *The Romantic Conception of Life: Science and Philosophy in the Age of Goethe* (Chicago: University of Chicago Press, 2002), p. 521.

12. *The Variorum Edition of the Complete Poems of Thomas Hardy*, ed., James Gibson (London: Macmillan, 1979). "Winter in Durnover Field," p. 149 and "The Darkling Thrush," p. 150.

13. In a later chapter I will be developing a further even more unlikely connection between Darwin and Hardy by focusing on their implications for the importance of the aesthetic. In Darwin's mindless world, as in Hardy's, the formlessness that would likely emerge from mindlessness is displaced by a powerful sense of the ordering force of the human mind – in Hardy more directly, in Darwin implicitly, the aesthetic plays a major role.

14. Charles Darwin, *The Descent of Man, and Selection in Relation to Sex* (Princeton: Princeton University Press, 1981 [1871]), p. 70.

15. *The Correspondence of Charles Darwin*. Vol. V: 1851–1855, ed., Frederick H. Burckhardt (Cambridge: Cambridge University Press, 1990), pp. 540, 543.

16. George Eliot, *The Mill on the Floss* (London: Penguin Books, 1979 [1860]), "Conclusion," p. 543.

17. Ruth Yeazell, *Art of the Everyday: Dutch Painting and the Realist Novel* (Princeton: Princeton University Press, 2008), p. 137.

18. William Archer, "Real Conversations," in Martin Ray, ed., *Thomas Hardy Remembered* (Aldershot: Ashgate, 2007 [1901]), p. 35.

3 *The Mayor of Casterbridge*

1. *Revelation*: 3:15–16.

2. George Eliot, *Daniel Deronda* (Oxford: Oxford University Press, 1984), ch. 68, p. 689.

3. Mary Shelley, *Frankenstein, or, The Modern Prometheus*, ed., M. K. Joseph (Oxford: Oxford University Press, 1969), ch. 24, p. 218.

4. Elizabeth-Jane, we read in the novel's penultimate paragraph, had "learned the secret . . . of making limited opportunities endurable" (ch. 45, p. 252).

5. Thomas Hardy, "The Profitable Reading of Fiction," in Ernest Brennecke, ed., *Life and Art: Essays, Notes and Letters* (New York: Greenberg, 1925), p. 73.

6. Florence Emily Hardy, *The Early Life of Thomas Hardy: 1840–1891* (London: Macmillan, 1928), pp. 193–194.

7. In Harold Orel, *Thomas Hardy's Personal Writings* (Lawrence, Kansas: University of Kansas Press, 1969), p. 39.

8. Thomas Hardy, "Candour in English Fiction," *Life and Art: Essays, Notes, and Letters* (New York: Greenberg, 1925), p. 76.

9. Northrop Frye, *Fables of Identity* (New York: Harcourt, Brace, 1963), p. 53.

10. Northrop Frye discusses this quality at length in *Anatomy of Criticism* (Princeton: Princeton University Press, 1957).

11. *Thomas Hardy's Personal Writings*, ed., Harold Orel (Kansas: University of Kansas Press, 1966), p. 134.

12. Frances O'Gorman, "Thomas Hardy and Realism," in Phillip Mallett, ed., *Thomas Hardy in Context* (Cambridge: Cambridge University Press, 2013), p. 117.

13. See, for example, H. M. Daleski, *Thomas Hardy and the Paradoxes of Love* (Columbia, MO: University of Missouri Press, 1997), p. 183.

14. *The Literary Notebooks of Thomas Hardy* (New York: New York University Press, 1985), Volume I, p. 140.

15. John Kucich, *The Power of Lies: Transgression in Victorian Fiction* (Ithaca: Cornell University Press, 1994).

16. See, for an interesting discussion of this connection, F. B. Pinion, *Thomas Hardy Art and Thought* (Totowa: Rowan and Littlefield, 1977). In his book on *Tess of the D'Urbervilles*, Dale Kramer emphasizes the way Pater's "impressionism," almost "pointillism," affected Hardy's style and intensified his own tendencies to see the natural world with the sort of enchanted particularity that I am arguing for in this book. See Dale Kramer, *Hardy: "Tess of the D'Urbervilles"* (Cambridge: Cambridge University Press, 1991), p. 31. See also Rosemarie Morgan, ed., *The Ashgate Research Companion to Thomas Hardy* (Ashgate: 2010), p. 95.

17. See my *Darwin the Writer* (Oxford: Oxford University Press, 2011).

4 From Mindless Matter to the Art of the Mind

1. In Hardy's poem "The Well-Beloved," the ideal figure tells the betrothed lover, who has hitherto seen his bride-to-be as the ideal, "I have ever stood as bride to groom,/I wed no mortal man." Hardy's very modern insistence on the personal nature of what the mind takes as objectively there makes the idea of a permanent *embodiment of* the ideal in nature chimerical. The ideal is never intrinsically in nature but the product of the lover's perception. When the lover sees his fiancée at the wedding, "her look was pinched and thin,/As if her soul had shrunk and died/And left a waste within."

2. J. Hillis Miller, "Modernist Hardy: Handwriting in *The Mayor of Casterbridge*," in Keith Wilson, ed., *A Companion to Thomas Hardy* (Chichester: Wiley Blackwell, 2009), p. 433 (henceforth CTH).

3. See Suzy Anger, "Naturalizing the Mind in the Victorian Novel: Consciousness in Wilkie Collins's *Poor Miss Finch* and Thomas Hardy's *Woodlanders – Two Case Studies*," in Lisa Rodensky, ed., *The Oxford Handbook of the Victorian Novel* (Oxford University Press: Oxford, 2013), pp. 483–506.

4. J. Hillis Miller, *Thomas Hardy: Distance and Desire* (Cambridge: Belknap, Harvard University Press, 1970), p. 4.

5. John Tyndall, "Science and Man," in *Fragments of Science* vol. II (New York: Appleton and Co., 1899), p. 358.
6. Thomas Hardy, in Lennart J. Bjork, ed., *Literary Notebooks* vol. I (New York: New York University Press, 1985) (henceforth LN), p. 95.
7. Walter Pater, *The Renaissance* (London: Macmillan and Co., 1888), p. 246.
8. For a general discussion of Hardy's views of art and of contemporary aesthetic writing, see Norman Page, "Art and Aesthetics," in Dale Kramer, ed., *The Cambridge Companion to Thomas Hardy* (Cambridge: Cambridge University Press, 1999). Page begins suggesting wide differences between Hardy's views and those of the contemporary aesthetic movement, but he concludes, having emphasized Hardy's eclectic inconsistencies and his emphasis on the idiosyncratic, "he may have more in common with the Aesthetic movement than has sometimes been supposed" (p. 52).
9. I have discussed this development in relation to Darwin in my *Darwin the Writer* (Oxford: Oxford University Press, 2009), ch. 4.
10. *Charles Darwin's Notebooks 1836–1844*, ed., Paul H. Barrett, Peter J. Gautrey, Sandra Herbert, David Kohn, & Sydney Smith (Ithaca: British Museum (Natural History), Cornell University Press, 1987), Notebook C, 266, p. 291.
11. *The Life and Letters of Charles Darwin*, ed., Francis Darwin (John Murray: London, 1887), vol. I, p. 316. The wonderful *Darwin Correspondence*, in process at Cambridge University Press, has not yet reached the last years of Darwin's life, so I cite the earlier publication of the letter.
12. Kay Young, *Theory, Interpretation, Narrative* (Athens, OH: Ohio State University Press, 2010).
13. W. K. Clifford, "On Some of the Conditions of Mental Development," *Lectures and Essays* (London: Macmillan, 1901), vol. 1, p. 79.
14. Quoted by Anger, p. 500, from Hardy's letter to *The New York World*, December 23, 1920 (*LW*, p. 441).
15. Thomas Hardy, *A Pair of Blue Eyes* (London: Macmillan, 1975), ch. 32, p. 345.

5 The Poetry of the Novels

1. Charles Darwin, *The Formation of Vegetable Mould through the Action of Worms with Observations on Their Habits* (London: John Murray, 1881).
2. John Bayley rightly notes "a sharp contrast in [Hardy's prose] between the physical perceptions, which are always his own, and opinions and ideas which seldom are" (pp. 17–18).
3. See Amy King, "The Divine Commonplace: Natural History, the Theology of Nature, and the Novel."

4. Charles Darwin, *The Voyage of the Beagle*, ed., Leonard Engel (New York: Anchor Books, 1963 [1839]), pp. 65–66.
5. For a valuable and thorough discussion of the importance to Hardy's imagination of astronomy, see Pamela Gossin, *Thomas Hardy's Novel Universe: Astronomy, Cosmology, and Gender in the Post-Darwinian World* (Aldershot: Ashgate, 2007). Anna Henchman discusses this problem of "parallax" in *The Starry Sky Within: Astronomy and the Reach of the Mind* (Oxford: Oxford University Press, 2014), pp. 24–31, and passim.
6. Gossin provides an extended analysis of the place of astronomy in the story in *Thomas Hardy's Novel Universe*, pp. 155–209.
7. Note another striking use of the perception of the sound of the wind through vegetation, this time in *Return of the Native*:

> Throughout the blowing of these plaintive November winds that note bore a great resemblance to the ruins of human song which remain to the throat of fourscore and ten. It was a worn whisper, dry and papery, and it brushed so distinctly across the ear that, by the accustomed, the material minutiae in which it originated could be realized as by touch. It was the united products of infinitesimal vegetable causes, and these were neither stems, leaves, fruit, blades, prickles, lichen, nor moss.
>
> They were the mummied heathbells of the past summer, originally tender and purple, now washed colourless by Michaelmas rains, and dried to dead skins by October suns. So low was an individual sound from these that a combination of hundreds only just emerged from silence, and the myriads of the whole declivity reached the woman's ear but as a shrivelled and intermittent recitative. Yet scarcely a single accent among the many afloat tonight could have such power to impress a listener with thoughts of its origin. One inwardly saw the infinity of those combined multitudes; and perceived that each of the tiny trumpets was seized on, entered, scoured and emerged from by the wind as thoroughly as if it were as vast as a crater. (Bk 1, ch. 6, p. 105)

8. Helen Macdonald, *H is for Hawk*. Kindle Edition. (New York: Grove/Atlantic, Inc., 2014), p. 273.

Suggestions for Further Reading

Bayley, John, *An Essay on Hardy* (New York: Cambridge University Press, 1978).

Björk, A. Lennart, ed., *The Literary Notebooks of Thomas Hardy* (London: Macmillan, 1985).

Boumelha, Penny, *Thomas Hardy and Women: Sexual Ideology and Narrative Form* (Brighton: Harvester Press, 1982).

Bullen, J. B., *The Expressive Eye: Fiction and Perception in the Work of Thomas Hardy* (Oxford: Clarendon University Press, 1986).

Butler, Lance St. John, ed., *Alternative Hardy* (New York: St. Martin's Press, 1989).

Cox, R. G., ed., *Thomas Hardy: The Critical Heritage* (London: Routledge, Kegan Paul, 1970).

Ebbatson, Roger, *Hardy: The Margin of the Unexpressed* (Sheffield: Sheffield Academic Press, 1993).

Garson, Marjorie, *Hardy's Fables of Integrity: Woman, Body, Text* (Oxford: Clarendon Press, 1991).

Gatrell, Simon, *Hardy the Creator: A Textual Biography* (Oxford: Clarendon University Press, 1988).

Goode, John, *Thomas Hardy: The Offensive Truth* (Oxford: Blackwell, 1988).

Gregor, Ian, *The Great Web: The Form of Hardy's Major Fiction* (London: Faber and Faber, 1974).

Hardy, Emma, *Some Recollections*, ed. Emma Hardy and Robert Gittings (London: Oxford University Press, 1961).

Howe, Irving, *Thomas Hardy* (New York: Collier, 1973).

Kramer, Dale, ed., *Critical Approaches to the Fiction of Thomas Hardy* (London: Macmillan Press, 1979).

Lawrence, D. H., "A Study of Thomas Hardy," in Edward D. McDonald, ed., *Phoenix: The Posthumous Papers of D. H. Lawrence* (London: Macmillan, 1985), pp. 398–516.

Mallett, Philip, ed., *Thomas Hardy: Texts and Contexts* (Basingstoke: Palgrave, 2002).

Meisel, Perry, *Thomas Hardy: The Return of the Repressed* (New Haven: Yale University Press, 1972).

Miller, J. Hillis, *Thomas Hardy: Distance and Desire* (Oxford: Oxford University Press, 1970).

Millgate, Michael, *Thomas Hardy: A Biography* (Oxford: Oxford University Press, 2004).

Morgan, Rosemarie, *Women and Sexuality in the Novels of Thomas Hardy* (London: Routledge, 1988).

Orel, Harold, ed., *Thomas Hardy's Personal Writings: Prefaces, Literary Opinions, Reminiscences* (London: Macmillan, 1966).

Purdy, Richard Liddle and Millgate, Michael, eds., *The Collected Letters of Thomas Hardy*, 7 vols. (Oxford: Clarendon Press, 1987–1988).

Taylor, H. Richard, ed., *The Personal Notebooks of Thomas Hardy* (London: Macmillan, 1979).

Wilson, Keith, ed., *A Companion to Thomas Hardy* (Chichester: Wiley-Blackwell, 2009).

Wilson, Keith, ed., *Thomas Hardy Reappraised: Essays in Honour of Michael Millgate* (Toronto: University of Toronto Press, 2006).

Widdowson, Peter, *Hardy in History: A Study in Literary Sociology* (New York: Routledge, 1989).

Widdowson, Peter, *On Thomas Hardy: Late Essays and Earlier* (London: Macmillan Press, Ltd., 1998).

Woolf, Virginia, "Thomas Hardy," in *The Second Common Reader* (New York: Harcourt, Brace and World, 1960 [1932]), pp. 222–234.

Index

Printed in the United States
By Bookmasters